Locked
in the Darkness

Retrieving a Hidden Girl's Identity
from the Holocaust

PREVIOUSLY PUBLISHED IN THIS SERIES BY YAD VASHEM:

Enzo Tayar, *Days of Rain*

Alan Elsner, *Guarded by Angels: How My Father and Uncle Survived Hitler and Cheated Stalin*

Isabelle Choko, Frances Irwin, Lotti Kahana-Aufleger, Margit Raab Kalina, Jane Lipski, *Stolen Youth: Five Women's Survival in the Holocaust*

Hadassah Rosensaft, *Yesterday, My Story*

Gabriel Mermall, Norbert J. Yasharoff, *By the Grace of Strangers: Two Boys' Rescue During the Holocaust*

E.H. (Dan) Kampelmacher, *Fighting for Survival*

Hersch Altman, *On the Fields of Loneliness*

Flora M. Singer, *Flora, I was but a Child*

Israel Cymlich, Oskar Strawczynski, *Escaping Hell in Treblinka*

Moty Stromer, *Memoirs of an Unfortunate Person: the Diary of Moty Stromer*

Menachem Katz, *Path of Hope*

Leib Reizer, *In the Struggle: Memoirs from Grodno and the Forests*

Mordechai Lensky, *A Physician Inside the Warsaw Ghetto*

Marcel Tuchman, *Remember, My Stories of Survival and Beyond*

Joseph Foxman, *In the Shadow of Death*

Leon Frim, *Seasons in the Dark, The Road from Przemysl to Nazi Hell*

PUBLISHED BY THE UNITED STATES HOLOCAUST MEMORIAL MUSEUM:

Adam Boren, *Journey Through the Inferno*

Margaret Bergmann Lambert, *By Leaps and Bounds*

Joseph E. Tenenbaum, *Legacy and Redemption: A Life Renewed*

Locked
in the Darkness

Retrieving a Hidden Girl's Identity
from the Holocaust

SABINA HELLER

YAD VASHEM AND
THE HOLOCAUST SURVIVORS' MEMOIRS PROJECT
New York • Jerusalem

This book is published by The Holocaust Survivors' Memoirs Project in association with the World Federation of Bergen-Belsen Associations, Inc.

The Holocaust Survivors' Memoirs Project, an initiative of Nobel Peace Prize laureate Elie Wiesel, was launched through a generous grant from Random House, Inc., New York, New York.

And

Yad Vashem, the Holocaust Martyrs' and Heroes' Remembrance Authority, c/o American Society for Yad Vashem, 500 Fifth Avenue, 42nd floor, New York, New York 10110-4299, and P.O.B. 3477, Jerusalem 91034, Israel

www.yadvashem.org

Cover photos and all other photographs courtesy of Sabina Heller

Library of Congress Cataloging-in-Publication Data

Heller, Sabina.
Locked in the darkness / by Sabina Heller.
p. cm.
ISBN 978-0-9814686-7-9 (alk. paper)
1. Heller, Sabina. 2. Adopted children--Israel--Biography. 3. Holocaust survivors--Israel--Biography. 4. Holocaust survivors--United States--Biography. 5. Jewish children in the Holocaust--Ukraine--Biography. I. Title.
HV874.82.H45A3 2012
940.53'18092--dc23
[B]
2012022292

ISBN 978-0-9814686-7-9

Typesetting: Judith Sternberg
Produced by Offset Nathan Shlomo Press

Printed in Jerusalem, Israel.

Publication of this book is made possible
by a generous grant from
Susan and David Edelstein

in loving memory of the family of Jakob Zylberberg

Scheindel Malka and Tovia Melech
Ethel, Sarah and Pearl
Avraham Meyer and Moishe Itzak

This book is dedicated to
The Kagans my biological parents
The Roztropowiczes my rescuers
Dr. Sophia and Zygmund Goszczewski my adoptive parents
Ron and Mark Heller my beloved sons

Language Editor: Leah Goldstein

TABLE OF CONTENTS

ACKNOWLEDGMENTS

I started writing my life story as a form of therapy in my efforts to cope with the discovery of my difficult past. In time, several people began to encourage me to turn these writings into a book.

My gratitude goes to my cousin Rachel Rabin Jacob, who changed my life by informing me about the materials available at the Jewish Historical Institute in Warsaw with regards to my early childhood during the Holocaust. My thanks also go to Carmela Cohen, who helped me find out important information about Yad Vashem, as well as to Dr. Hezi and Ruti Rutenberg, who helped me organize my initial thoughts.

My special thanks go to Kevin Norwood, who taught me computer skills and later encouraged me and assisted me with editing my book.

I am also indebted to Martin Lesak from the CAA agency for his valuable and constructive criticism and guidance. My dear principal and friend Sally Shane helped me in proofreading and editing.

My gratitude also goes to Yad Vashem for their assistance, in particular to Dr. David Silberklang and Daniella Zaidman-Maurer for their invaluable advice.

I thank my dearest friend, Prof. Abraham Sion, for his important input and support in the writing of this book.

Most of all, I am grateful to Ron and Mark Heller, my beloved sons. They were always there for me when I struggled with my past. Their love and support kept me going until this work was complete – and beyond.

FOREWORD

By Robert Krell, M.D.

Sabina (Inka) Heller arrived in Israel in 1950 at the age of eight with her parents, Dr. Sophia and Zygmund Goszczewski. Her name changes from Inka Kagan to Inka Goszczewski, and at that point, "her life begins." She has no memory of the early years of her existence. In fact, Sophia and Zygmund Goszczewski are actually the third set of adults to take meaningful responsibility for her, but the only ones she can recall.

How is it possible to lose all memory of so many years? And why does it happen? This is not my first encounter with such a claim from someone who survived the Shoah at a young age. It is for good reason that Sabina and others like her found it impossible to evoke the events they experienced at the time. It allows them to live in the present, and even shape a possible future. However, Sabina, like many other child survivors, recognizes the presence of a "deep sadness and a constant sense of loss." She states, "I always felt different."

I know something of that feeling of sadness and loss. It accompanies those of us who were given into hiding, passed off to strangers, without the ability to understand the circumstances. That understanding came much, much later. Meanwhile, we felt forever rejected by our parents, not knowing that they acted out of love and selflessness, or indeed committed an act of courage no parent should ever be forced to contemplate: the giving up of a child in order that he or she may have a chance to live. And even with that supreme sacrifice, only a comparative handful of Jewish children survived the ordeal of Nazi persecution.

Born in 1941, Sabina was rescued from immediate danger at only nine months old, but she was soon abandoned, left to die of starvation and cold by her caretakers who had grown tired of the responsibility. A miraculous rescue by a sixteen-year-old girl, Zosia Stramska, brought her to the home of her new family, Józef and Natalia Roztropowicz and their three teenage daughters and young son, who nourished the skeletal infant back to health and kept her safe for the remainder of the war. They decided not to conceal Inka Kagan, instead presenting her as "the child of their slain cousins." Fortunately, Inka did not "look Jewish."

It should be noted that Sabina, like other very young Holocaust survivors, defies the theories of psychological development. Widely agreed-upon scientific understanding holds that a child requires nourishment, security, a nurturing parenting figure, warmth and love for at least two years in order to have a reasonable start to a healthful and normal life. Few of these requirements were available to Inka until close to the end of her second year.

Prewar psychologists and psychiatrists emphasized the catastrophic effects of even one major trauma in early childhood, and advocated prolonged and intensive therapy to help with the healing process. But when Jewish children emerged from many years of experiencing chronic deprivations and massive psychological and physical trauma, somehow the same healers absented themselves from the postwar scene. In fact, as in the case of children and adolescents found at the Buchenwald concentration camp, young survivors were described by mental health professionals as psychopaths – who else could have been able to survive the camps? Far from psychopaths, that particular group produced a future chief rabbi of Israel, Rabbi Israel Meir Lau, and a Nobel Peace Prize laureate, Elie Wiesel, as well as politicians, physicists, doctors, teachers, successful businesspeople and loving homemakers.

Sabina herself achieved a life created from the slimmest of the usual necessary ingredients. That achievement still requires examination by the relevant professionals. How in fact did these children recover in order to live meaningful lives?

This book documents Sabina's search into her past stimulated by the discovery of a file on her in the archives of the Jewish Historical Institute in Warsaw. With this information, she was able to trace the fragments of memory that eluded her both because of her tender age and her need to suppress the memories of the traumatic separations and appalling conditions of her infancy.

After saving her life, the Roztropowiczes performed a second righteous act. They returned her to a Jewish orphanage so that she could reconnect with her people. This incredible sacrifice of the child they loved as their own caused a second hugely traumatic separation for Inka to endure. But it, too, was an act of devotion and courage, perhaps as much as the initial sacrifice by her natural parents. Later in life, Sabina learned of the depths of the attachments of those who cared for her. Natalia Roztropowicz sent letters to the orphanage that went unanswered. She pleaded for information. Her love and commitment are ever evident.

This powerful memoir chronicles the experience of only one child of many whose lives were similarly shaped in the cauldron of Jew-hatred now known as the Shoah. They are children with distorted roots, fragmented memories and deformed identities. They could have easily fallen by the wayside of social reintegration, but most did not. Like Sabina, they pursued normality with a hunger that those who have lived a normal life simply do not possess. Dear reader, you will be forever enriched by delving into these pages, and absorbing the struggle and courage of one such child.

Robert Krell is Professor Emeritus of Psychiatry at the University of British Columbia, Vancouver. He was a hidden child in The Hague, Holland.

FOREWORD

By Rachel Rabin Jacob

Six million Jews perished during the Holocaust, a huge number that is difficult for a human being to comprehend, but one survivor's story changes all this, and enables us to begin to understand the depth of this human tragedy.

Naturally, we in Israel heard all about the plight of the Jews in Europe.

The Shoah became personal to me when my cousin Zosia (Sophia), her husband Zygmund and their daughter Inka arrived in Israel, after surviving the horrors in the ghetto and camps. Their story made the Shoah very real and impossible to forget.

My father, Nehemiah Rabin, brought them from the temporary tent housing in the *maabara* to stay with him until they settled down. This is when I saw Inka for the first time – a cute, blue-eyed, eight-year-old blonde girl. She smiled and seemed very friendly, even though we could not communicate because she did not yet speak Hebrew.

From time to time on my visits to my father I noticed the changes in her. She learned Hebrew, made friends and slowly transformed into a *sabra*. She even lost her Polish accent and adopted the Israeli pronunciation in Hebrew.

When she visited us in Kibbutz Manara during her summer vacations I saw a normal young girl. There was no trace of the child survivor of the Shoah. Inka developed like any Israeli girl – elementary school, high school, service in the IDF, marriage. When she married, she moved with her husband to Los Angeles. She raised a family and never spoke of her past. She lived in the present and seemed to enjoy life.

In one of our chats, she told me that she did not remember anything of her early childhood except being with a Polish family for several years and going with them to church.

I also recall a conversation with Zosia regarding Inka's adoption. After the war Zosia, a physician, volunteered to work in the orphanage and decided to adopt a child. She adopted Inka. However, Inka had no idea she was adopted; Zosia never revealed this to her.

I felt this was wrong and that Inka should be told the truth. Zosia disagreed. She was adamant that Inka should never find out about the adoption. Zosia made it very clear that this decision was final, not given to any further discussion. I dropped the subject and never brought it up again.

Everyone in Inka's parents' circle knew that Inka was adopted, but respected Zosia's wishes not to tell Inka. So Inka grew up convinced that Zosia and Zygmund were her biological parents.

When Zosia passed away, while returning to the hotel in my car back after the funeral, Inka confessed that since she did not remember anything from her past. She said she would like to find out about her childhood, but she did not know how to go about it. I kept quiet and just listened to her.

One night I received a phone call from Dr. Emunah Nachmany Gafny, who came upon Inka's case in the Jewish Historical Institute in Warsaw while working on her PhD dissertation. What should I do? Should I tell Inka the truth or not? That was the question.

Finally, I decided to tell Inka about this new information about her and let her decide whether she wanted to pursue it. She made it clear to me she wanted to know everything there was in that folder about her. She called the Jewish Historical Institute and for the first time received all the information about her past. She was finally able to fill in the huge gap in her memory.

Inka showed strength of character in dealing with her discoveries. She went through several stages, from the initial shock to anger for being kept in the dark about her adoption and past to acceptance. She started writing about her experiences to ease the pain. This was therapeutic and eventually turned into a memoir.

This memoir gives us a glimpse into the strength of the human spirit, which enables us, after experiencing hell, to build a new life, raise a family with love and hope, and lead a normal life.

CHAPTER 1

Funerals

C lutching a eulogy I am about to deliver, I find myself scared and alone. I look around the cemetery in Holon, Israel, where my mother is about to be buried. The weather is miserable – wet, cold and gloomy – matching my mood. Even though friends and family surround me, I still feel alone. My cousin Rachel Rabin is standing next to me, but her warmth and kindness aren't enough to chase the loneliness away.

Mom's final wish was to be buried in Israel, next to Dad. I am still exhausted from the 20-hour flight from my Los Angeles home to honor her last request. I feel numb, and not just from jet lag. I am compelled to follow the Jewish custom of burying the dead immediately, but everything is happening so quickly. I cannot absorb it all.

It is the end of an era for me. My mother was my last tie to the country in which I grew up. She was my role model. Sophia Goszczewski was ahead of her time. She was a professional at a time when women rarely worked outside the home. She was an excellent doctor, a loyal friend, a great human being and a loving mother.

I look around me and see the people who have come to pay their last respects. I have not seen most of them for thirty years. They have aged, but they are all here. They did not forget my mother, even though she had lived in the US for her last twelve years. Sophia was still their heroine from the Lodz ghetto and the concentration camps.

After the funeral, I ask Rachel to drive me back to my hotel. We drive through the streets of Tel Aviv. In a flash, memories of my youth came pouring back.

Tel Aviv is not a huge city. I used to walk everywhere. I knew every house, every tree, every stone. In spite of all the changes, much of the city's character stayed the same. Like a small version of New York, the streets were full of bustling people, with cafes on every corner. It is hot and humid just like in the Big Apple, but Tel Aviv is in the Middle East, so there are also falafel stands with their unique aroma, narrow curvy streets with outdoor bazaars, and the ever-present Mediterranean Sea.

Rachel pulled into the Dan Panorama Hotel's parking lot. We walked into the elegant lobby of one of Tel Aviv's newest hotels along the Mediterranean beach. We decided to sit down and have some tea at the coffee shop.

Rachel and I both were in a reflective mood. I turned to her and said, "I remember arriving in Israel as an eight-year-old girl. It seems like a dream now. It is hard to believe that forty-seven years have passed since then."

Rachel smiled and said, "I remember your weird-looking hairdo when you arrived. No offense!"

"Not only was my hairdo weird, so were my clothes. I had a strange accent. I felt like a person from another planet." I remembered how desperate I was to get rid of the Polish-girl image and become a *sabra* – a native Israeli.

Rachel's voice brought me back from thinking about the past. "Inka, your Mom sat and talked to me for hours about the horrors she endured in the concentration camps. But she never mentioned in those heart-to-heart talks how she had saved so many lives as a doctor. It was only later that I found out from her wartime friends what a heroine she really was. She was a remarkable, amazing woman, way ahead of her time! Everyone admired her."

I remembered everything about our life in Israel – the good times and the bad. "Do you know, Rachel, what part of my life I miss the most? The first eight years. It's a black hole. I don't remember anything at all. As far as I'm concerned, my life started at the age of eight, when I arrived in Israel. I never really had the time to deal with it; I was young and I wanted to live my life and not dwell on the past. However now, as I near 60, I would really like to find out more about my early childhood. It is very important to me now. But the truth is, I don't know where to begin."

Rachel sat quietly listening, sensing my anguish. She made no comment as I went on, "I am so frustrated not knowing or remembering anything about my past. When my parents were alive, we never talked about these things. I never persisted, even though I often thought about it. Now I really want to know! I would like to make some inquiries, but I have no idea how to go about it," I added with a sigh. Rachel kept silent and then abruptly changed to a lighter subject – our dinner plans for that evening.

After sitting *Shiva* (the Jewish seven days of mourning), I returned home to Los Angeles to be with my sick husband, Alfred, who had been battling emphysema for two years, and my sons, Mark and Ron. Two weeks after my mother's funeral, Alfred passed away.

Even though my mother and husband had both been very sick for a long time, their deaths were terrible blows. I had taken care of both of them for years. However, it was comforting to know that they didn't have to suffer anymore.

But now that they were gone, I felt a terrible void. This was the first time in my adult life that I was completely on my own. I have never lived on my own, as many young American women do. I had gone from my parents' home to my husband's. I had never experienced being on my own. What kept me going were my sons Mark and Ron. They were young men in their twenties. They still needed me. Looking back, I don't know who needed more guidance, they or I.

At 57 and widowed, I threw myself into work teaching at public school, and it helped. It provided some structure to my life. But I still had to struggle with making difficult decisions on my own, and getting used to life as a single woman.

I took the new challenge like a trooper. I needed to make economic decisions that were going to affect our lives. I plunged into educating myself about finances and investments. I read books and talked to people knowledgeable in these areas. Mark helped me as well. Slowly my sons and I settled into our routines. Life seemed to be moving at a more normal pace without the roller coaster crises we had experienced during the tragic last year of my husband's sickness.

I was about to find out that life is full of surprises.

CHAPTER 2

Phone Calls and Mail

It was an ordinary November evening at home. I had just finished washing the dinner dishes and feeding my dog Roxie. I took a shower, and then wrapped myself with my warm blue robe that Mark had given me for Hanukkah. I was getting ready to collapse into my favorite chair to watch my favorite sitcom, when the phone rang.

I looked at my watch; it was 11 pm – too late for my friends to call. I picked up the phone. It was a long distance call from Israel. I heard Rachel's voice speaking in Hebrew.

"Hi, Inka. Do you remember our conversation after the funeral?" she asked.

I was not following her. "Regarding what?"

"Do you remember your wish to know more about your early childhood?"

"Yes, I remember."

"A moment ago, I received a phone call from a lady named Emunah. She has just come back from Poland. She has found a lot of information about you."

I was astonished. I had to sit down. "Who is Emunah, and how did she get hold of information about me?"

"Emunah is an Israeli doing research for her Ph.D. about hidden chil-

25

dren during the Holocaust. She went to the Jewish Historical Institute in Warsaw, Poland."[1]

"So where do I fit in?"

"This is what happened. One day while she was searching in the Institute's archives, the Institute's director, a Mr. Reisner, walked in smiling. He was holding a manila folder, which he kept glancing at. Aware that Emunah was from Israel, he asked, 'Have you ever heard the name Inka Kagan?' Emunah shook her head.

'I hoped it might ring a bell.'

When Emunah asked why he was asking, Reisner replied:

'She's a child survivor from the Holocaust; I thought it might interest you. I just received a folder full of documents from a Polish woman named Ms. Roztropowicz–Szkubel. Her parents rescued a Jewish girl during the war years. They searched for her for fifty years, but couldn't find her. Recently, they decided to give the documents about Inka to us. I'd love to find Inka and unite her with her wartime family.'

'It sounds interesting and I wish I could help you find her, but I can't. I've got to work on my dissertation. I hope you understand,' replied Emunah."

"How did Emunah get in touch with you then?" I persisted, out of curiosity.

"It's a long story that I'll tell you another time," Rachel replied. "What's important is whether you really want the information, which might include things you did not know. I want you to think about it and call me whenever you're ready."

That night I could not sleep. I kept thinking about what Rachel had told me. I felt as if somebody up there had heard my wish. It could not be just a coincidence. Some greater force was listening and trying to help me.

I had mixed feelings. One part of me was scared of the unknown. Who knew what I would find? Another part of me was pleading, saying it was time to know the truth, no matter what!

I wondered what was in the folder. Did it really hold the secret of my

---

1   The reference is to Dr. Emunah Nachmany Gafny. Her dissertation has been published in Hebrew and English as *Dividing Hearts: The Removal of Jewish Children from Gentile Homes in Poland in the Immediate Post-Holocaust Years* (Jerusalem: Yad Vashem, 2009). [ed.]

first eight years? I wanted to find out everything there was to know about those years. I needed that information to complete my life. I needed to fill the gap.

The next day I called Rachel. "Yes! I must know what's in the folder. Please tell me what I need to do to get hold of it!"

I emphasized my determination to face the information awaiting me. I wrote down the phone number of the Jewish Historical Institute in Warsaw, Poland, whose work on Jewish survivors in the immediate postwar years in Poland was funded by the Lauder Foundation, created by the family of Estee Lauder, founder of the giant cosmetic company.

To my great relief, Mr. Yale Reisner answered the phone in English. I was in such a frenzied emotional state that I could not possibly converse in Polish, even though Polish was the language I had spoken to my parents in Israel. But that was nearly thirty years ago. I was no longer fluent.

I introduced myself and explained that I lived in the US and was extremely anxious to find out what was in the mysterious folder. He was very understanding and cooperative. He suggested I write a formal request letter to him, and he would photocopy all the documents and mail them to me. He offered to translate all documents from Polish into English before sending them on.

Time dragged for the next two weeks. I checked my mailbox twice a day, but nothing came. All I could think of was the mail from Poland. When was it going to arrive?

Then one morning, as I was returning from the grocery store holding a heavy grocery bag, I heard the phone ringing. In a rush of adrenaline, I slammed the front door with my foot, dropped the bag on the floor with all the groceries falling out, and rushed to the phone.

I picked up the receiver and heard a male voice. "Mrs. Heller, this is Mr. Reisner from the Jewish Historical Institute. I wanted to talk to you before you receive the package of documents I sent you. I was in touch with your cousin Rachel in Israel. She is very concerned about you. I want to tell you certain things about your life that you don't know. It's very awkward to do so over the phone, but I will try to be as gentle as possible."

He paused for a moment. "In 1948, a Jewish couple, Zygmund and Sophia Goszczewski in Lodz, Poland, adopted a six-year-old girl named Inka Kagan from a Jewish orphanage. Inka Kagan became Inka Goszczewski overnight. In 1950 they immigrated with Inka to Israel, and settled in Tel Aviv." As he was explaining, it suddenly hit me that he was talking about me.

"They, the Goszczewskis, never told you about the Roztropowicz family who rescued you from death during the war. The Roztropowicz family never forgot you. They looked for you for fifty years. In 1999 they finally gave up, and turned over all the documents they had kept about you to our Institute."

It was a bombshell! This was the first time I had heard that I was adopted. I was in complete shock. I couldn't believe what I was hearing.

I tried to listen attentively to Mr. Reisner's explanation, but at some point I could not focus on what he was saying. The palms of my hands were sweaty. My heart was racing. I was exhausted. I don't remember hanging up. I felt a weakness in my knees and I dragged myself to bed, where I lay down and stared at the ceiling. I was alone at home and felt so lonely. I did not have any of the people I loved around me to comfort me. My parents were dead. My husband was dead, and my children were somewhere going about their lives. I was 57 years old, and my life had just been turned upside down.

I wanted to cry, but I felt numb.

I began to ponder: who am I? Who were my biological parents? How come they never told me I was adopted? All these years, and not a word. I had a right to know the truth. Maybe they wanted to spare me the pain when I was a little girl. But what about later on, when I became an adult; they should have told me then. *They Should Have Told Me!* What were they thinking? Didn't they realize that one day I would find out? Wouldn't it have been better if they were the ones who had told me the truth rather than my having to hear it from a total stranger over the phone? Here I was, alone with all these questions, and no one could answer them. They had taken their secret with them to their grave.

Zygmund and Sophia were the only parents I had ever known. They had loved me, and I them. I missed them. I was so confused by the different emotions I was feeling. I was a wreck!

I looked around me. On my desk was a picture of Ron and Mark. It brought me back to reality. Should I call them to share my discovery? Sooner or later I would have to tell them, but not quite yet.

I wondered, "How will my sons react to this news? Will they respect me less? Will the fact that I was adopted affect their sense of identity?"

After recovering from the initial shock, I was ready to tell my sons about the news of my adoption. I talked to each one separately. Ron, my eldest, who always took interest in our family history, wanted to know all the details. I could not answer all his questions; I simply told him what I knew so far. Mark listened silently. When I finished my story, he hugged me and said he loved me. That was what I really needed.

Ron and Mark shared in the discovery process of my past. They witnessed the initial jolt I experienced when I learned about the horrors of my formative years. They saw the pain and agony on my face when I heard about being adopted. They felt my anger and frustration at never being told about my adoption. I felt as if I had been living a life based on lies. They were outraged that I had been intentionally denied the truth. They tried to support me as best they could. Ron, a history buff, plunged into studying and researching the Holocaust in Eastern Europe, particularly Ukraine. He became an expert in this subject. When I decided to put my story to paper, he helped me with the research. Mark, who is four years younger, was studying biology at college and tried to concentrate on his schoolwork.

At times they did not know how to respond. What can you say to a mother when her world collapses?

Sometimes I would cry for no reason at all. I felt my old melancholy creeping up, threatening to take over my life. I felt so alone. That deep sadness and a constant sense of loss emerged again and again. I had always felt different. Now I knew it was because I *was* different. Maybe that was why I was never truly happy.

Then fury took the place of sorrow! I was mad at Zygmund and Sophia. But I could not vent my anger because they were dead.

The only person who could shed some light, who might have had some answers, was Rachel. I called her and shared my frustrations and anger towards my parents. Rachel, who had known my parents and me from the day we arrived in Israel, was silent for a few seconds. Then she said, slowly, "We all knew you were adopted. Everybody who knew Zygmund and Sophia during the war years was well aware of your adoption! The family and all their friends kept it quiet. They were respectful of your parents' wishes. *Everybody knew except you."*

I felt even worse than before. There had been a conspiracy to prevent me from knowing the truth!

Once the package arrived, reality struck. I struggled with conflicting emotions: I wanted to know, and yet I was afraid of what I might discover. My hands were shaking as I opened the large, brown envelope and slowly pulled out a big folder.

The first page was a picture of Natalia Roztropowicz, my Polish mother, with a little girl I guessed to be me. I stared at the photo for a long time. It was the first time I had seen a picture of myself so young. I had often wondered about my looks as a little girl. Was I pretty? Was I cute? What kind of hair did I have?

Now, after all those years, I had a chance to see myself. It felt like I was getting to know a new person. I *was* a cute little girl. It also brought back memories. I stared at the photo of Natalia. I could remember how attached I was to her, how much I loved her. My eyes filled with tears. I now got in touch with a part of me that had been dormant for a long time. It felt good. I had found a part of me that was missing – like a mislaid piece of a puzzle.

My life had not started at the age of eight, after all. I *did* have a childhood.

I gazed again at the photo. It was a very moving moment. I saw a four-year-old with a kind of "Shirley Temple" look. I had big, blue eyes, lots of blonde, curly hair with a bow on top, and a serious little round face. I wore a short dress with long sleeves and a white apron over the top. I wore thick stockings to keep me warm. I was standing next to Natalia, slightly leaning on her. Natalia was sitting on a chair. Her face was very stern. She was wearing big round glasses. Her black, straight hair was pulled back and tied in a bun. She wore a black sweater and a dark, simple skirt. Under the photo, a handwritten caption said "Natalia Roztropowicz with her wartime daughter – Inka Kagan, Nidzica, 1945."

This somber photo, in a way, reflects the grave mood of the times. It was not a cheerful picture. The photo is in black and white – more black than white. We both look very serious; there was none of the carefree childish happiness that a little girl my age would usually display.

I put down the picture of Natalia and me and started to read the summary of my life, which Mr. Reisner had been kind enough to translate for me. It felt very strange, like reading a mystery book about another person.

As I read, there were new revelations in every sentence. My last name had been changed several times during my life, depending with whom I was living. How about my place of birth? All my life I was under the impression

Natalia and Inka, first photo Inka saw as
she opened the folder of her past.

that I had been born in Poland. Now I discovered that I was only partially correct. I was born in what is now Ukraine.

There are certain basic facts about life that one simply takes for granted,
such as first and last name, birth date, place of birth, etc. This basic information appears on any I.D. card. When asked, the answer is automatic. A person
does not need to think – it is who you are. Everything I knew to be true turned
out to be false. Who was I?

I started to search for anything that would help me understand my past.
I went over to the drawer where I kept memorabilia and old documents. I started to move around some old yellow papers that were falling apart. There was
my faded I.D. card from the time I served in the Israeli army, my discharge
papers, my father's I.D. card, issued when we arrived in Israel, and a tarnished

photo of my mother's brother, who had perished in the Holocaust. Suddenly I came upon a birth certificate. My eyes lit up with excitement. It was *my* birth certificate. I let out a sigh of relief. Now I would learn the truth. Slowly I began to read, but the information did not match the facts I knew.

Only my first name and birth date seemed to be correct. It said that my name was Sabina Goszczewski, the family name of my adoptive parents. But the place of birth was not Lodz as I expected it to be, because that is where Zygmund and Sophia were from, but Radziwiłłów.

From what I now know, my adoptive parents had never lived there. My birth certificate was not helpful in clarifying who my biological parents were. On the contrary, it showed how complicated my past was. It was not my real birth certificate. It was a fake! It had been issued in Lodz after the war, with Zygmund and Sophia Goszczewski putting themselves down as my biological parents. After the war, Poland was in ruins. Valuable documents were destroyed. Millions of people were moved from one country to another. In that state of turmoil, it was possible to fabricate "facts" that were not necessarily true. There was no reliable way to verify the truth. That is how I believe my birth certificate was created. I continued reading, and every page yielded new information. The folder I received included many documents from my past. One of the documents was regarding religion.

There was no doubt in my mind about my religion. Not only was I Jewish, I grew up in Israel. I was a proud Jew! I consider myself almost a *sabra*. But when I looked at the documents I received from the Jewish Historical Institute, I was shocked to find a certificate that stated I had been baptized in a Catholic church! I was even more confused now. I decided to return to the documents I received from the Institute. It dawned on me how little I knew about Ukraine in the years before the war, during the war and afterwards. Actually, I didn't know anything at all. All I knew was that Ukraine had been a part of the Soviet Union. Where it was exactly, I hadn't the faintest idea. The Soviet Union did not exist anymore. Ukraine was now an independent country.

I feverishly looked for a world atlas. I found the continent of Europe. There was Poland, and just east of Poland I found Ukraine. Then how come I spoke Polish and not Ukrainian?

My mind went back to the photo of Natalia and me. Maybe the answer lay there. I looked at it again. Instead of answers, I had more questions. Who was she? Was she Polish or Ukrainian? How was I related to her? I needed to know more about her and her family. After carefully reading the documents in the folder, this is what I learned about Ukraine and the Roztropowicz family:

Ukraine as we know it now did not exist before World War II. At that time, it was divided between the Soviet Union and Poland. The Soviet Union occupied the eastern parts of Poland in September 1939, including Polish Volhynia (Wolyn), which now became Soviet Western Ukraine. The Germans invaded and occupied the area in June 1941.

The Roztropowiczes were a Polish family who lived in Soviet Eastern Ukraine. They were not happy under the Communist regime, so in 1925 they decided to cross the border to Western Ukraine in order to improve their quality of life. All they wanted was to make a living and raise their children in peace. But there were many forces at work in the area beyond their control, and they were prevented from realizing their wish. The Ukrainians hated the Polish authorities, and resented the Jews who were in the middle. That explains why I spoke Polish living in Ukraine. Still the question remained: assuming I was Jewish, how did a Jewish baby end up with a Polish Catholic family?

The western Ukrainians wanted self-rule. The Nazis understood the tensions that existed among the different ethnic groups and used them to their advantage, and into that climate I was born.

Once the Germans arrived, they followed the same pattern as in every other town or village they conquered in soviet territories regarding their treatment of the Jewish population. First they shot Jews on the streets and later systematically at prepared killing sites; later they enclosed the Jews in ghettos, where they suffered from starvation and repeated raids; and finally they deported the remaining Jews to mass murder sites.

Radziwiłłów was no exception!

I returned to the atlas, feeling more confident that finding the town of Radziwiłłów would be easy. I put on my glasses. My finger made a path from west to east and from north to south. I could not find anything that resembled this name. It was very frustrating! I checked other maps, but there was no mention of a city by that name. I was determined to get to the bottom of this mystery, but how?

I talked to my friends, and they suggested I go to the local Los Angeles Museum of the Holocaust, which might be able to help me. Accompanied by my sister-in-law and a friend, I went to the Museum, then located on Wilshire

Boulevard. As soon as I explained my problem to the staff, they understood the cause of my confusion. They suggested I look at a different map.

It was a map of Ukraine from before 1939. I realized that the borders had changed after 1945, at the end of the war. I was looking at the wrong map. I felt a surge of relief. I looked at the old map. But Radziwiłłów did not appear there either. After further investigation, I discovered that Radziwiłłów was close to Brody. Brody was on the map! I was born in such a tiny place, it did not even appear on a map!

CHAPTER 3

The Kagans

The following day I looked at the documents again, and made more discoveries. It was the first time I learned about my biological parents – Mr. and Mrs. Kagan. They had named me Sabina when I was born, which was later shortened to the endearment Inka.

I felt a sharp pain in my chest as I read this. I was fifty-seven years old, and I had just found out the last name of my biological parents. I realized I did not know anything about them, except that they were Jewish. Were they alive or dead? What were their first names? Who were they? What did they look like? What happened to them? Did I look like my father or my mother? Whom did I take after? Did I have any siblings? Were there still any people alive who could answer some of my questions?

If my parents were the Kagans, then how did I end up with the Roztropowicz family? In a letter that Natalia Roztropowicz addressed to me, she made an attempt to give me some information about how I ended up with them during the war.

The Kagans' first names are unknown. They lived in a village named Radziwiłłów in what was Poland then and is Ukraine today. The town consisted of three ethnic groups – Poles, Ukrainians and Jews. The Poles and Ukrainians were mostly farmers. The Jews earned a living from the small industries that processed the agricultural produce.

I learned that my grandfather, whom they called Kishel, had a grain mill. My biological parents lived separately from the Poles and Ukrainians in a community of their own. Józef Roztropowicz, a Polish farmer, used to bring his produce to my grandfather's mill. The Roztropowicz family knew my grandfather only from doing business with him. It was strictly a business relationship. A beautiful blonde woman would sometimes come to the mill. Kishel would point her out to Mr. Roztropowicz and declare proudly, "That is my daughter!" He was referring to my biological mother!

From the information I received, I was most likely their only child, and lived with the Kagans in the ghetto for the first nine months of my life.

As with many East European ghettos at that time, our ghetto was sealed from the outside world. The living conditions inside were appalling and unbearable. Many people were crammed into tiny apartments. Food was scarce. The young and healthy would work for the Germans. But with the hard work and little food they did not last long. The harsh winter in Ukraine, combined with the fact that there was no fuel to keep them warm, also took a heavy toll on the population in the ghetto and many died.

Putting Jews into these crowded, inhuman conditions made the job of mass murder much easier. The Ukrainians would catch Jews who wandered out of the ghetto, drag them to the outskirts of the city, order them to dig a ditch and shoot them right there.

In May 1942, rumors spread in the ghetto that the Germans were planning another deportation raid.[2]

I am guessing that the following scenario would have occurred when the Kagans, like many families in the ghetto, faced macabre choices that no human being should have to make. I can imagine my parents having a heated argument when they learned about it.

My father would have approached the sensitive subject cautiously. He might have said to my mother, "You know that the Germans are planning an-

---

2   The Radziwiłłów ghetto was closed on April 9, 1942, with 2,600 Jews in two ghettos, one for "useful" Jews and one for all the others. The 1,500 Jews in the latter ghetto were murdered on May 29, 1942. The Jews of the "useful" ghetto were murdered on October 6, 1942. A small number of Jews managed to find hiding places in the area, mostly among local Baptists. See Guy Miron and Shlomit Shulhani, eds., *The Yad Vashem Encyclopedia of the Ghettos during the Holocaust* (Jerusalem: Yad Vashem, 2009), pp. 640–641. [ed.]

other *aktzia* [murder operation] in our ghetto. When they find out we have a baby, we are all going to die."

"Yes. I was thinking about that. What do you think we should do?"

"We can stay here and wait to see what happens, or we can use our connections with our non-Jewish friends."

"How? Do you have a plan?"

"We will escape the ghetto at night by bribing the guards and find shelter with a non-Jewish family; we'll pay them to provide us a hiding place in their house."

"Suppose we do escape – what if the sheltering family finds the situation too risky for them? What if they kick us out? What will we do then?"

"In that case, we'll leave little Inka with them. This is the only way she might survive!"

"You mean, leave our baby with strangers? I can't even think about it! How do you expect me to do that?"

"We need to try, or it's certain death for all of us."

I imagine that my mother started to sob uncontrollably. She went over to the crib where baby Inka was napping. As she gazed at the peacefully sleeping child she was grateful that the baby was too small to understand the cruel, evil world that surrounded her. I can picture her being up all night. There would not have been much time to waste. She had to make a decision as soon as possible. She reached the agonizing decision that there was no other choice but to do what her husband had suggested.

The Kagans held a bundle of their belongings and nine-month-old baby Inka in their arms. They made their way out of the ghetto to the "Aryan side," where the Miszczak family hid them in their attic.

Many Jews could not believe the unbelievable stories about mass murder. Some parents who still had a chance to send their children away refused to separate from them, and unwittingly sentenced them to death.

This single brave decision of the Kagans was about to save my life. My parents' connections with the leaders of the Polish community – the police and the Catholic Church – proved to be of help at this moment of desperation.

I was curious about the Miszczak family and why they agreed to hide my parents. Here is what I found out from the documents. Mr. Miszczak was a Polish policeman. Maybe the parish priest, Father Brodecki, approached Mr. Miszczak with an offer from the Kagans to hide them in his house. The offer may have included money and other valuables as compensation for the risk of hiding Jews. Mr. Miszczak might have hesitated and asked for time to consult his wife on the matter. Perhaps Mr. Miszczak was leaning toward accepting my parents' proposal. He had probably never seen so much money in his entire life. The Miszczaks were living on his small police salary. His wife was unlikely to be enthusiastic about the idea. She knew that the burden of caring for me would fall on her shoulders. She was also likely worried about her family's safety, especially that of her two teenage daughters. She may have been totally against the Kagans moving in also out of fear of what the neighbors would say when they would see wet diapers hanging on the clothesline.

Of course, at that time, there were no clothes dryers or disposable diapers. In fact, there were no diapers! Instead they used bed sheets cut into squares.

After the heated discussions, Mr. Miszczak finally prevailed, noting what the money from the Kagans could do for their family, especially their two daughters, who might need dowries soon. This could be their chance to secure their daughters' future and also improve their own lives with better food and clothing. Father Brodecki then worked out the details of the agreement, and was a witness to the transaction.

Hiding Jews was punishable by death. The Miszczak family felt forced to reconsider their offer and asked my parents to leave. The Kagans pleaded with them to rescue their baby, little Inka. The Miszczaks agreed to care only for the baby.

Most probably the Kagans did not return to the ghetto because that meant certain death. They did not have many options. There were very few people they could have counted on. They heard that there was a farmer who had a large barn in which he let a Jew hide. They were determined to go there and find shelter. It was also close to the Miszczaks. This way they could still inquire about their daughter.

I would like to think that when the Kagans entered the barn, they were surprised to find many people they knew from their community. The place was crowded – it was not meant for that many persons. It was little more than a wooden shack. But with all these familiar faces, it felt safe. They undoubtedly sensed they had made the right decision going there.

The farmer would come in at night and bring them some food and drink. They gave him everything they managed to save – money, jewelry, clothes and shoes. They were all very grateful to him for giving them shelter because getting caught outside would have meant the end.

Jewish life had little value during the war. Since the Germans did not know who the Jews of the community were, they depended on local villagers to help them find them and turn them in. The Nazi regime offered the local population a reward of three liters of vodka for every Jewish head.

I imagine that my parents and the others huddled together, trying to support each other with words of reassurance that this too would pass – they would manage to survive and return to normal life. With this in mind, my parents found a spot, spread their blanket, and prayed for a peaceful night. Perhaps they did not fall asleep for a while. It was the time of night when left to their own thoughts, the horror of their existence dawned on them.

Ukrainian collaborators terrorized the area. Word reached the bandits that Jews were hiding in the barn. The collaborators set it on fire, killing every person inside. The Kagans were burned alive in that fire. They disappeared from the face of the earth leaving no trace – no grave to mark their final resting place.

That was the night that changed baby Inka's life forever. She was nine months old. Her future at that moment seemed very bleak; her chances for survival had been significantly reduced. From then on, she would be at the mercy of strangers.

CHAPTER 4

The Cellar

With the death of the Kagans, the Miszczaks' source of income dried up. It became increasingly dangerous to live on their farm on the outskirts of Radziwiłłów. The Germans were everywhere. Many families were forced to vacate certain rooms in their homes for German officers to move in. Besides the Germans, families like the Miszczaks faced a dangerous threat from the Ukrainians, who hated the Poles. Poles were murdered daily.

In this climate, the Miszczaks were hiding me, a Jewish baby and were less than thrilled about it. Mrs. Miszczak was particularly unhappy caring for the baby. Conditions on the farm were very primitive. There was no indoor plumbing in the house. Every time water was needed, they had to bring it from the well. They did not have electricity. For light, they used gas lamps. Waking up several times a night to feed Inka was a hardship. As long as the Kagans were alive and the money had flowed in, the Miszczaks had taken good care of Inka. After the Kagans perished in the fire, everything changed. Inka became a burden, and a risk to the entire family. Mrs. Miszczak resented all the extra work involved in caring for Inka. They wanted to get rid of her, but they did not know a good way to do it without posing a danger to themselves. They took off and left baby Inka unattended, alone in the house.

Among the documents I received was a diary written by Natalia's daughter, Stanka. From the diary, I learned that the Miszczaks had left me in a dark cellar, without food or heat in the freezing East European winter. They were hoping that I would not survive this ordeal, that somehow I would disappear, either through natural death or perhaps by the Ukrainians setting the house afire, disposing of me. The Miszczaks stayed in Radziwiłłów for seven days, and to their great surprise, when they returned they found the house intact with Inka still very much alive. I guess an angel must have been watching over me.

The situation on the farm deteriorated daily. It became clear to the Poles living there that they needed to move to a safer area permanently. The Miszczaks and I moved to an apartment in Radziwiłłów.

Radziwiłłów was more modern. Apartments had plumbing and electricity. Some businesses even had telephones. The apartment in which the Miszczaks settled was very small – one room for the parents and one tiny room for the two daughters. There was just enough room for the two beds. The Miszczak daughters complained about having to share a bedroom and fought endlessly. The kitchen had to be shared with another family, the Stramskis – a widower, a son, and a daughter named Zosia. The mother had died at a young age.

In the kitchen, behind the ceramic stove far from sight, was a tiny door that led to a dark, cold cellar. The cellar had no windows. Usually a place like that was used to store food for the winter, because it was the coldest area in the apartment. It was the next best thing to a refrigerator. The low temperatures there prevented food from spoiling.

That is where they put Inka. It was an excellent hiding place, but hardly suitable for a nursery. Inka was kept there day and night. Mr. Miszczak was away most of the time, working long shifts in the police station. It was Mrs. Miszczak who was in charge of Inka's care. She had an idea regarding what to do with that Jewish baby girl. She had a friend build a custom wooden bed. They drilled holes in the bottom of the bed and covered the holes with hay. All the baby's waste would go down to the floor, so Mrs. Miszczak would not have to bother with diapers. Needless to say, Inka lay in that bed without any clothes, covered only with a purple blanket.

This arrangement freed Mrs. Miszczak to do whatever she pleased. It is possible that Inka cried at first. But when her crying did not produce any results and nobody showed up to bring her a bottle of milk or cereal or show her any kind of attention, Inka stopped crying. To expedite her death, Mrs. Miszczak stopped giving her food or drink, hoping that in a short time she would become weaker and weaker and eventually die of starvation. Inka just sat there in the dark, day in and day out, hungry and abandoned in the freezing cold cellar. Nobody knew of her existence. She was doomed to die.

Then one day a miracle happened.

CHAPTER 5

Zosia Stramska

Zosia Stramska was a sixteen-year-old Polish girl who spent much time cooking in the kitchen her family shared with the Miszczaks. One morning, Mrs. Miszczak went out to the local bazaar to buy food, Mr. Miszczak was at the police station, and his two daughters were out with two German soldiers, keeping them company, so Zosia she was in the kitchen alone. This is Zosia's account of how she found Inka, as described by Natalia in her letter.

Zosia was alone in the house. She stepped into the kitchen to make breakfast, enjoying a quiet moment having the house all to herself. She placed a cup of coffee and a slice of bread on the kitchen table. As she walked over to the stove to warm her cold hands, she heard a feeble noise coming from the direction of the stove. She was puzzled.

She was about to sit down when she noticed a tiny door. Wondering what was behind the door, she opened it quietly, peering into the room behind it. It was dark and cold. Gradually her eyes adjusted to the darkness. She walked in, and was hit by a terrible odor.

As she carefully felt her way in the darkness, she saw the shadow of a little creature rocking back and forth. Next to the wall was a wooden crib, and inside was a baby girl – or what used to be a baby. The baby looked like a skeleton. Her skin was hanging off her skeleton; you could see her bones through the almost transparent skin. She was dehydrated. She was not crying. All Zosia could see were her eyes – big, blue eyes, pleading for help.

The little emaciated child was completely naked, lying in her own waste. There was a filthy little blanket in the corner of the crib.

The horrible odor filled the air. Zosia could smell death. The little baby was moving her body in a constant rocking motion. She did not move her head. Only her eyes reacted to the ray of light when Zosia entered the cellar. Her tiny hands were like sticks. She had long nails. Her dirty hair was all tangled and messy. The baby was not going to last much longer in these inhuman conditions. She was dying a slow, painful death right before Zosia's eyes.

Zosia was horrified by her discovery. Obviously this was a well-kept secret, and nobody was supposed to know about it. She ran to the kitchen and returned with the soft part of the bread and some milk diluted with water. She let the child drink a little swallow at the time, and handed her small pieces of bread. Zosia was very cautious not to give the baby too much food, so the child would not become sick. She watched the child devour the food. It was apparent that the child had not eaten anything in a very long time.

Suddenly, Zosia heard some voices outside. She left the cellar in a hurry and closed the door. She did not want anyone to know that she had uncovered the hiding place of the child.

"She must be Jewish!" Zosia thought to herself. "That is why her existence is shrouded in such secrecy."

Zosia lost her appetite for breakfast. She cleaned the kitchen table, and rushed to her room. She did not feel like talking to anyone. She was so moved by the sight of the little infant being starved to death that she could not face anybody. She just wanted to be by herself with her own thoughts. She had to calm down, in order not to give away her frantic state of mind.

Many ideas went through her head. The worst thing she could do was act impulsively. She decided to sneak some food to the child whenever possible, until a better and more permanent solution could be found. That night, Zosia did not sleep much. She tossed and turned, unable to relax at the vision of the baby locked up in the back of the kitchen.

She woke up early, feeling worn out and stayed in bed a while longer, wondering with whom she could trust her discovery. She thought of her best friend Stanka Roztropowicz. She knew her family well. She saw them at many church functions. They had invited her to their house many times.

Zosia secretly envied Stanka for having such wonderful parents. These were times when she sorely missed her own mother. The Roztropowiczes were so warm and caring, and she knew she could share her secret with them.

CHAPTER 6

The Roztropowicz Family

From left standing: Jana, Zosia, Stanka
Seated: Natalia, Jendryk, Józef, 1938

I do not remember much about the Roztropowicz family, but here is what I learned from the documents I received. They were a family of six: the mother Natalia; the father Józef; the daughters Zosia (19); Jana (Janka) (16); and Stanka (15); and the son Jendryk (7). Józef sold his farm produce in the bazaar, bringing home the remains for his family's consumption. The Germans had taken Zosia Roztropowicz to Germany for forced labor.

Natalia was a devoted wife and mother. She was able to keep the family going even during the horrific circumstances of war. Natalia was a devout Catholic. It must have been her religion that sustained her through the most horrendous time in human history. She faced difficult situations in a calm, collected manner. She was smart, resourceful and determined.

Zosia Stramska did not regret telling the Roztropowicz family about her discovery. Natalia said she had heard rumors about a baby being mistreated and kept in inhuman conditions, but she did not know the details. Zosia promised that when the next opportunity arose and she was alone in the apartment, she would call Natalia to come and see the child with her own eyes.

Zosia waited for the right moment to take Natalia and her daughters to see the baby. That moment came sooner than she expected.

Mrs. Miszczak and her daughter, Milka, were getting ready to go to Brody, a large city in the region. Zosia was spying on them. Once they left, Zosia ran as fast as she could to the Roztropowiczes' house (of course, there were no telephones). She entered the house breathless, her cheeks flushed from running, and found Natalia busy in the kitchen, and Stanka working out in the garden.

When Stanka came into the house, she was annoyed at the interruption; she was passionate about gardening. "What is so important? There is still a lot of work to be done!" she blurted out.

Zosia said in a low voice, "Remember the baby I was telling you about? I want you to see for yourself the unspeakable conditions in which she is being kept. I can show her to you right now, because no one is home."

She didn't have to say another word. Natalia, Jana and Stanka immediately joined Zosia, and ran to Inka's hiding place.

The door was unlocked. The long, dark hallway led to the kitchen. There was a strong odor of perfume coming from the bedroom of one of the daughters. Pictures of Jesus and other saints were hanging along the hallway. A picture of the Virgin Mary was displayed in the corner. The kitchen was a mess. Somebody had eaten breakfast in a hurry and had left behind dirty cups of tea and plates covered with breadcrumbs. There was nothing unusual about the scene. "Where could they possibly have hidden a baby?" asked Natalia.

Then Zosia pointed to a small door beside the stove, almost hidden from sight. She opened the door softly, so as not to frighten the child, and let them in. Natalia, Stanka and Janka were speechless. Natalia had never seen such a horrible sight. In her letter to me, Natalia described the scene:

> For as long as I live, I will never forget what I saw. I am pretty tough, but the vision sent shockwaves through my entire body. I saw a corpse; her hair standing on end, her eyes bulging, her neck like a thin stick, and her hands with long nails that curled upwards. She looked like a skeleton. She hardly moved. She was sitting in a small wooden cradle, in the bottom of which were holes covered with straw. The urine ran down to the floor through the holes, while the excrement remained on the straw.
>
> When a ray of light entered through the open door, she did not blink her eyes, but something moved – maybe I imagined it, but it seemed she called "Mama!" Maybe it was my imagination, because she did not know how to talk yet. In any case, we decided then and there to take her with us. I could feel her breath as I cradled her under my coat.[3]

Natalia sent Stanka and Janka home quickly and asked them to fill up the tub with warm water. All of a sudden Natalia stopped in her tracks. A thought flashed through her mind. "What if the child looks Jewish? That could put the whole family at risk." "Well, it's too late now," Natalia mumbled as she entered her house.

Once home, Natalia put the baby in the tub and washed her little body with soap and water very carefully. They shampooed her hair and dried her fragile body carefully with a soft towel. They had to dry her very tenderly because her skin was so delicate. Finally, Natalia put the child on the couch.

They took a deep breath feeling a great relief. Inka had beautiful curly blond hair, big blue eyes, and a cute little nose. There was nothing Jewish about her. Nobody would imagine she was Jewish.

3   The full text of Natalia's letter is in Appendix 1.

Inka sat on the couch without moving her head. Her eyes were getting used to light. Only her pupils moved, checking the room and the people.

They did not have any baby clothes. How were they going to dress little Inka? They started searching for some fabric. Maybe they could manage to put together an outfit for her. Unfortunately they could not find any material. With the war going on, the stores were not open and basic materials were in short supply. Then, Stanka said, "What about the dolls?"

Nobody knew what she was talking about. Stanka exclaimed, "Inka is so skinny and tiny we can dress her in our doll's dress!"

She turned to her sisters, checking for their reaction. It was a great idea! They decided to try their doll's dress on Inka. It fit her perfectly. Being blonde, she looked adorable in the doll's tiny blue dress. Inka was their new doll!

Jana describes Inka's condition when they brought her to their family:

> It was desperate. She could not walk, because she was too weak and because no one had taught her. Her bladder was running all the time. She had tuberculosis. She had diarrhea and she was de-hydrated. Her body was covered with rashes. She had a terrible fear of being left alone, and could never be left in the darkness. She would go into convulsions. She didn't cry. We had to teach her to cry. Natalia set up a routine for Inka's care. We had two shifts. At night, Natalia took care of the child. During the day, Stanka and Janka cared for her. She needed constant attention – just like in intensive care.[4]

Stanka mentions in her diary[5] how they had to feed Inka every hour and change the dressings on her sores. She describes how they taught her how to walk and talk. They cooked foods for her that were very nutritious. It was lucky that the Roztropowiczes were farmers. They grew potatoes and other vegetables. They also had fruit trees, so they were able to provide Inka with fruits and veg-etables. They also had a cow, which meant they had milk and dairy products.

4   From Janina's letter to Yad Vashem's Department of the Righteous Among the Nations in 2002, Yad Vashem Archives, M.31/8980. [ed.]
5   For excerpts from Stanka's diary see Appendix 2.

The Roztropowicz family had a meeting to discuss the best way to ensure their safety with the presence of Inka. After a heated discussion, Natalia's strategy prevailed. They decided not to hide Inka. On the contrary, they were going to take Inka out in the open, to the community, and introduce her as the child of their slain cousins. There was nothing about her that could give away the fact that she was Jewish. She did not look Jewish. Inka was just learning to talk, so she hadn't developed a Yiddish accent. It was a credible story at that time, since Ukrainian nationalists were persecuting Poles to the point that many Polish people had been brutally murdered.

Soon the Roztropowicz family settled into a routine, with Inka playing an important part. In many ways, the presence of an innocent child, unaware of the war's brutal events, was good for the family. Her laughter, her playful ways, and her awkward attempts at learning to walk and talk all helped relieve the tension, and even brought about some worry-free moments.

Inka regained her health slowly, and was oblivious to the changes taking place at the Roztropowicz residence. The German headquarters had notified the Roztropowicz family that a German officer would be moving into their house. They were to vacate one room in the house for him.

This was good news and bad news. The bad news was that there would be less living space for their family. They would also need to watch their conversations when he was around. The good news was that whenever a German officer moved in with a local family, the family felt a lot safer, the officer's presence offering them protection. Nevertheless, the Roztropowicz family was very apprehensive about the new tenant. They did not know what changes his presence might bring to the family.

It turned out that their fears were unjustified. The officer, Otto, seldom came to the house. He was polite and intelligent. He frequently brought candies for Inka. It never crossed his mind that the little girl he liked so much was Jewish.

Still, dangers lurked everywhere for the Roztropowicz family. The Nazi regime was cruel and repressive. The Nazis considered the Poles subhuman and treated them as slaves, as did the Ukrainian nationalists. Józef would tell his children to carry sand in their pockets. In case of an attack, they were to throw sand in the eyes of the attacker and run away as fast as they could.

The Roztropowiczes took other measures to protect the family. The children slept in the back room, which was close to a forest. In case of emergency, they were to jump out the rear window and then run and hide in the forest behind the house until the danger had passed. Józef and Natalia were always on alert. At night, they took turns keeping watch to make sure that no one approached the house with destructive intentions.

It was a daily struggle to survive. In her diary, however, Stanka explains that the decision to rescue Inka under these circumstances did not seem so difficult. After all, they were exposed to life-threatening situations daily. It just seemed like the right thing to do.

While life was very strenuous, there were funny moments as well.

One evening after dinner, while the family was relaxing together with Herr Otto, he took out his harmonica. When Inka saw it, she ran and got her toy harmonica. Herr Otto started to play, and so did Inka. She was convinced that it was her toy harmonica that was producing the sounds. She looked very silly, making funny faces while playing. Herr Otto seemed to be enjoying this comical situation. How would he have reacted if he had known that the little girl entertaining him was Jewish?

A few months later, the Roztropowiczes were notified that another German soldier would be moving in with them. They had to move out of their bedroom and sleep in the kitchen. Natalia slept with Inka in one bed, and Jendryk slept in a bed next to them. Eleven people now slept in the Roztropowicz household every night.

By this time, the Soviets were approaching Radziwiłłów. The Roztropowiczes were located in an area that was fast becoming a battlefield between the Soviets and the Germans. Hidden in trenches, the Germans were shooting all the time. While the fighting continued, the Roztropowicz family was left without electricity. The wind blew through the broken windows that had been shattered by the bombardments in the area.

CHAPTER 7

Liberation

On March 19, 1944, the Soviets liberated Radziwiłłów. The Roztropowiczes watched the German troops retreat. It was a happy day – a day they never believed they'd live to see. They were free at last!

Even though the war was over, the battles still continued. The Germans had retreated to a forest between Radziwiłłów and Brody, and formed a front. The Soviets sent more troops to conquer the German fortifications. The local population was ordered to retreat to the town of Białao Krynica. The Soviet Army occupied most of the houses, so the Roztropowiczes found a stable in which cows were being kept and moved in.

Natalia and Józef decided to go to the town of Dubno in the northeast, where Natalia's parents lived. The family loaded their few belongings onto a horse and wagon for the short trip. Józef had found horses abandoned by the Soviets because they were badly wounded; he took them and nursed them back to health. Natalia rode in the cart with me (I was two years and eight months old) while the other members of the family walked.

As they were walking beside the cart, the teenagers were bored to death. Gustek, a neighboring 17-year-old youth, confessed to Jana that he was in love with Stanka. He told her he wanted to write her a letter, but was hesitant because he was too shy. Jana offered to help. She dictated a love letter to Stanka using the most passionate words she knew to express Gustek's feelings.

The letter never reached Stanka, but fell into Natalia's hands. As she read it, her face turned pale and her expression furious. Jana keenly observed the developing situation. She felt compelled to tell her mother that it was in fact she that had written the unfortunate letter. By doing so, she saved the innocent Stanka and Gustek from a lot of trouble. Natalia turned to Jana and said with a menacing voice, "Don't ever do that again!"

This kind of silly game was totally unacceptable within their strict Catholic upbringing. I am sure that Natalia's firm old-world religious beliefs influenced my future development.

The Roztropowiczes arrived at the home of the grandparents in Dubno and settled in. One afternoon, Józef came home visibly annoyed. He reported: "The word is out that the repatriation of all the Poles in Ukraine back to Poland will start in a week! We will probably be moved to a place somewhere in the north of Poland. The rumor is we will be going by train. We can take whatever we need. There are no restrictions. We need to start packing right away."

After this announcement, Józef slammed the door and left.

Natalia was overwhelmed by the news. She was born in Ukraine. True, she was a Pole living in Ukraine, but she felt at home. Her family lived there. Her friends and neighbors were there. This war had ruined their lives and was continuing to uproot her and her family, throwing them into the unknown.

Natalia's mind drifted to her five children. How would they react to the news? It was going to be a hardship for all of them.

A noise at the door brought her back to reality. It was Stanka. Natalia told her to call the children. She needed to break the news to them.

CHAPTER 8

On the Train to Nidzica, Poland

In her diary, Stanka describes the morning the Roztropowiczes left Ukraine to be repatriated in Poland. They said their goodbyes to Natalia's parents in Dubno. Everyone was teary-eyed and emotionally drained. In their hearts, they knew that they'd never see one another again. Traveling was not what it is today. Everyone except Inka carried his or her belongings in a suitcase. Natalia inspected the house to make sure nothing was left behind.

The only cheerful person in the family was Inka. She was unaware of what was going on. They made their way to the train station on a horse and buggy. When they arrived, the station was crowded with fellow Poles facing the same destiny. There was an atmosphere of quiet resignation. Here and there they saw a familiar face. That was comforting.

At the appointed time, the train pulled into the station. But instead of passenger cars it was comprised of freight cars! Comfort was not a priority. Nevertheless, people immediately started to board the train, pushing and shoving, afraid of being separated. Families desperately tried to stay together. At the same time, they were anxious to load their earthly possessions with them.

Three hours later, the doors of the train slammed shut and we began our long ride to Poland. There was one small oven in the corner of the freight car. Each family took turns cooking their food in the oven. There was one oil lamp – no electricity. When the lamp went out, everyone sat in the dark.

As Stanka describes in her diary, they traveled for two weeks – day and night – without stopping. They never got off the train. They lost track of time.

The trip seemed to last forever. To pass the time, the family read books during daylight, played games and made plans for the future. The food supplies started to dwindle. Without refrigeration, the sandwiches that had tasted fresh and delicious at first became soggy and warm.

Rumors spread that they were going to Nidzica in northern Poland, an area previously populated by Germans. However, the Germans had been forced to move back to Germany, so we were going to live in the houses they had vacated. This was good news, as Germans were known to take good care of their homes.

The sleepy, tiny town of Nidzica was situated next to a large forest. From the distance, we could see small houses surrounded by gardens. The houses were separated by dirt roads with German names. It was a ghost town. Towering over the town was the church.

Józef, Stanka, Jana and Jendryk went in search of the right house for the family. Józef turned down the children's choice to live in a medieval castle outside of Nidzica. The children wanted to pretend they were Polish nobility.

Instead, Józef found a more practical solution, a house near the forest suitable for his family. The officials changed the name of the street from a German name to the Polish word for forest, which made the family feel more at home. They took a deep breath before entering the house. It was not huge, but it was adequate. The children were going to share rooms. One bathroom for seven people is not convenient, but they learned to cope.

The house was almost empty, except for a table with broken chairs left behind by the previous occupants.

The Roztropowicz children took off to explore the neighborhood. They ran from house to house, looking for things that could be useful in their new home. They lacked all the basic items. All they possessed were some clothing and bed linens. They needed kitchen utensils, pots, pans, dishes and furniture. Nobody had any money. Anyway, there was nothing to buy and nobody to buy it from.

The older children immediately realized the important role they played in ensuring the family's survival. Sometimes, while wandering around Nidzica, they would discover the corpse of a soldier lying amidst the ruins. Stanka wrote: "It was quite a shocking experience. The war events made us wiser than our age. We had to grow up fast in order to survive!"

The house had some land around it, suitable for a garden. This was very important. Józef planned to grow fruit and vegetables there. This would become their food supply.

It was not an estate, but it all was theirs now! The Roztropowicz family was excited and ready to begin a new life. At the same time, they realized that no one from Inka's family had survived the war, and they decided to keep her permanently in their family and raise her as their own child. Inka was baptized in a Catholic Church and renamed Irena Roztropowicz. A document of the baptism was included in the folder I received from Warsaw.

The Roztropowicz family enrolled Inka at a school. I do remember the trauma of going to school that first day, but I was so attached to Natalia that I would literally cling to her neck all the time. I was frightened of being away from her and I felt safe only when I was with her. Any kind of separation was unthinkable to me. Walking alone to school was a terrifying experience. I had to cross a field that seemed so huge, and I felt danger lurking at every turn. I cried and cried. In the end, however, I learned to go to school like everybody else.

I remember little else of that period. There are a few hazy images, such as the fear on that first day of school. Another of my recollections is praying with the priest at the beginning of each school day. A scene that stayed with me was the priest placing a wafer in my mouth after the Sunday sermon. It was a kind of beginning of normal life for the Roztropowicz family. What I did not know was that for me, normal life in Nidzica was not going to last long.

The Roztropowiczes told me about an incident that happened to Inka. One day, Inka came home from school crying. Natalia hugged and kissed her and asked what had happened. With tears running down her cheeks, Inka replied, "My friends keep calling me an orphan Jewess! Why do they call me a Jewess? I am not a Jewess! I am not an orphan!"

Inka was mortified by the idea that she might be Jewish. Since Jews were still stereotyped in the classic antisemitic terms in Poland, she felt offended to be portrayed as one. Natalia became painfully aware that she would not be able to shield Inka forever from the hostile environment that still existed in the Catholic community toward Jews.

Inka's baptism, the Church of Saint Wojciech,
Nidzica, July 15, 1945. Standing left: Inka,
second man from left Józef Roztropowicz;
standing right: Natalia

CHAPTER 9

Natalia's Dilemma

At about that time, the Jewish community in Poland became aware of the plight of the hundreds of hidden children in Poland that had been raised as Christians in monasteries and with Catholic families.

After the war, this issue of the hidden Jewish children had been brought to the attention of two organizations, the Jewish Agency for Palestine and the World Jewish Congress in the United States, by Jewish soldiers within the liberating armies of the Allies. The Jewish Agency sent agents to Poland to help find a way to retrieve these hidden children and return them to the Jewish community. The result was the establishment of an organization called the Zionist-run *Koordynacja* – the Coordinating Committee for Redemption of Jewish Children in Poland. Its goal was to redeem the children by offering monetary compensation for their care. They then placed the children in children's homes, where they would get some Jewish education, and eventually brought them to settle in Israel.

At its inception, the Koordynacja dealt only with Polish Jewish children, but later they also included "repatriated" children from the Soviet Union. I fell under that category.

Natalia relates in her letter that after the war, she and Józef made it known that they had hidden a Jewish girl. They hoped that someone from Inka's family had survived, and would come looking for her. The news about a Jewish hidden child in Nidzica reached the main office of the Koordynacja in Lodz. They decided to send a representative named Yehuda Bornstein to

Nidzica to talk to the Roztropowicz family about the child. Yehuda wrote a letter to the Roztropowicz family, advising them of his scheduled arrival in Nidzica the following week.

On the appointed morning, the tall skinny man with curly hair and a friendly smile showed up at the Roztropowicz home. Yehuda introduced himself and noticed little Inka making the bed. He then commented that he was there to discuss her future.

Yehuda gazed at the room in which they were sitting. He saw a large family of seven people (Zosia had returned) in a tiny, crowded house, struggling to survive. He noticed the mismatched teacups and plates from which Natalia served the refreshments. The clothes the family members were wearing were clean and well ironed but noticeably worn from frequent laundering. The collection of mismatched furniture needed repair.

Yehuda began by saying: "I came to tell you how grateful the Jewish community is for the brave act of kindness you showed to a Jewish baby during the dark days of terror. People like you restore my faith in the human race.

"You knew Inka's parents. They were good, decent, Jewish people. You know that were they alive today, they would want little Inka to be brought up among her own people, don't you?"

Natalia responded, "That is true. But, sadly they are not alive. I feel that Inka is part of our family now. It might harm her to be separated from us again. We are the only family she has ever known. It might set her back. We love her. We care about what happens to her. She has suffered enough."

"I know you love her and care about her. But all the love in this family cannot protect her from a hostile and anti-Jewish community. How will you feel when she returns from school crying because another child called her a dirty Jew?" answered Yehuda.

"How do we know what will happen to our Inka if we let you take her from us? We don't want to lose her," said Natalia, her voice reflecting her enormous motherly concern.

"I can give you my word that you will always be informed about Inka's whereabouts. We understand you're worried about her fate. Our community wants to compensate you for your expenses in caring for Inka through the war years. It is not a great amount of money, but it can help you. Of course, what you have done can never be measured in monetary terms. We realize that."

Yehuda stopped. He felt he had said enough for one day. He pleaded with Natalia to give it serious consideration. He promised to be back in a week.

Yehuda did not expect the Roztropowicz family to be receptive to his idea. Being an agent of the Koordynacja was dangerous at times. There were a few incidents in which families who sheltered children had gotten so attached to them that the parents refused even to consider giving them up. Sometimes they resorted to violence, and threatened the agent with a gun if he showed up again at their house. It was a very emotional issue, and extreme caution and understanding were needed in dealing with these families. Still, Yehuda knew he had planted the seeds with the Roztropowiczes. He decided to leave, and give the family time to consider their options.

One morning early the following week, Yehuda arrived once more at the Roztropowicz household. Stanka opened the door and said in a low, stern voice, "My parents are expecting you in the dining room."

Yehuda entered the room and found the whole family sitting around the table. The mood was somber; there was great tension in the air. Natalia's eyes were red. She looked exhausted after struggling with this heart-wrenching decision. She spoke for the family.

Turning to Yehuda she said: "After long deliberations and soul search-ing, we have come to the decision that Inka's destiny is with her people. I can honestly say that our main concern is her happiness. When some Jews who were passing through Radziwiłłów approached us, offering to take her, we refused. We care about what happens to her. I hope she won't hold this deci-sion against us. We love her and we'll miss her terribly. I am going to write a letter to her, and explain to her our decision as best as I can. We will hand this letter to her when she grows up. I hope she will be able to understand our decision better."

Natalia then left the room in a hurry, holding back her tears until she was out of sight. Józef took care of all the formalities. It was agreed that once Natalia had brought Inka to the orphanage in Lodz, the Roztropowicz family would be compensated with a certain amount of money for taking care of her during the war.

CHAPTER 10

The Orphanage

A couple of weeks after the final meeting with Yehuda, Natalia said to me, "Today is a special day. We are traveling to the big city of Lodz!" I was very excited.

I vaguely remember the trip, mainly because it was my first time on a train. It was a new, overwhelming experience. I was completely unaware of what was about to happen.

It was also the first time I tasted an orange. I thought it was the sweetest and most delicious thing I had ever tasted. I don't remember anything else. I have no recollection of arriving in Lodz, or how I got to the orphanage. It seems all hazy and wrapped in fog.

One of the documents is a receipt from the Koordynacja, stating: "We hereby confirm that the citizen Natalia Roztropowicz turned over to us a Jewish girl named Sabina Kagan, whom they rescued and cared for during the Nazi occupation. During her stay with them they named her Irena Roztropowicz." Natalia dropped Inka off at the orphanage and disappeared without even saying goodbye. I assume that in my effort to deal with the new situation in which I found myself, I erased her from my memory. With her departure, the first six years of my life faded into oblivion.

I understand that Natalia left in a hurry without any explanation because she was advised to do by the Koordynacja. Maybe she preferred it that way too – it was less painful. It is possible that everybody felt that under the circumstances, this was the easiest way – just drop the child off in the orphanage and walk out without making a big fuss. I suppose they thought it best for both parties involved.

However, I don't think it was best for me. In fact, I am convinced it was bad for me. It left me with a sense of abandonment that stayed with me for years to come. People were constantly coming into and going out of my life. I was never given a reason. It left me perplexed and confused. It contributed to my insecurity with a sense that something unpredictable might happen to me at any given moment. I developed a great fear of the unknown, which has remained with me through the years.

Who knows what went through my mind at the orphanage? I was six years old, and my world as I had known it had just collapsed. Enclosed with the documents I received from Yale Reisner were letters, postcards and pictures I had drawn. In the letters I wrote home, I addressed the Rostrpowiczes as Mom and Dad. I inquired when they would come and visit me. Maybe I thought that my being in the orphanage was a temporary situation, like a summer camp, and when summer was over I would return to the Roztropowicz family.

Once in the orphanage, Yehuda Bornstein showered me with attention. He bought me a doll – the very first doll that was truly mine. I loved that doll. I had never had any toys before. That doll was so important; she provided me with a sense of security. She was my constant companion. I held on to her. Wherever I went, the doll went with me. I slept with her. I ate with her. I played with her, and I talked to her. I never let go of her. She was the one thing that was not going to leave me.

It turned out that this doll was very therapeutic for the situation in which I had found myself. Today, many child psychotherapists use dolls when dealing with a child suffering from trauma.

I do have clearer recollections from the orphanage. I guess I arrived in the spring, because soon after my arrival we had a big party, a Purim party. I received some photos from that party in the orphanage. I had the part of a clown in a play.

In the orphanage, I did things I had never done before. We went on trips

Photos from the orphanage in Lodz, 1948-1949

Inka, bottom row center

Purim, Inka center

Hanukkah, Inka far left

to a forest where we had picnics. At night we had pillow fights in the girls' bedroom. Yehuda took me with three other girls to a photographer. He bought us ice cream and took us to the movies. I was overwhelmed. These were all incredibly exciting experiences for me. I must have felt like Alice in Wonderland.

There were so many changes, and everything happened so fast. I no longer went to church or recited my prayers kneeling next to my bed, praying to Jesus. No longer did I have to do chores around the house. Yet, at the same time, I no longer had parents, three sisters and a brother.

Among the documents I received were letters I had written to the Roztropowicz family during my time at the orphanage.[6] I wrote one to Stanka, dated October 20, 1948.

> My dear!
> I received the letter from you and I thank you very much. I am well here and I'm going to school. I was at the movies and in the park. I got a beautiful doll. It's nice here. I play with my friends. What are my friends back home up to? Please ask Daddy and Mommy to write when they arrive.
> > I kiss you strongly,
> > > Inka

On December 13, 1948 I wrote to Natalia and Józef:

> Dear Mommy and Daddy,
> Why doesn't Jana write to me? Is Januszek [Jendryk] going to come visit us? Stanka came to see me. Can Mommy come visit? I'm doing fine here, having a lot of fun playing with the kids. I'm coming home with Stanka for vacation. Is everyone well? Where are Daddy and Jana working? I would very much like it if Mommy could send some material to Stanka in Warsaw, because she's going to sew dresses for my doll.
> I kiss my parents on the hands and Jana on the mouth,

6   The letters below are all from the collection of documents that Yale Reisner sent to Sabina Heller in October 1999. The originals are in the archive of the Jewish Historical Institute in Warsaw. [ed]

Inka

Not all the letters I received in the file were full of such childish innocence. There was a letter from a woman named Teresa. I assume Teresa was one of the women working at the orphanage, and she was responding to one of Natalia's letters inquiring about my whereabouts:

Dear Madam,

I'm terribly sorry that I have not answered you for so long, but I had a lot of work to do. Now I am on vacation, so I can write. Inka did not cry at all. Inka came to me in the kitchen in the morning and asked if Mommy left. When I said yes, she smiled, left the kitchen and went off to play with the kids. A few days ago, I asked if she wanted to go to Mommy and she said it was very nice here and she didn't want to go. I was very surprised; she's an odd character – there's never been a child like that who hasn't cried for her mother. The man who brought her bought her a very pretty doll, and she walks around with it very happily, just as if she had been born and raised here. Once, the director came and said, "Teresa, what a polite child that is: she never cries, she never seems homesick." So don't worry about her, because she's doing quite well here and everyone here loves her, because she's so well behaved.

I send heartfelt greetings to you and please do not be angry at me because I did not write back very quickly.

Teresa

I do not know if Natalia was angry at Teresa, but she was certainly upset with the Koordynacja. She mailed this strongly worded letter to the Committee on September 8, 1949, but it was sent back to her, marked "return to sender."

Although my letters continue to go unanswered, I turn to the Committee once more with the following question: Please let me know about the child that I returned to the Jewish community one year ago, namely Inka Kagan (Roztropowicz). From our side, we've lived up to our agreement, i.e. we have gradually withdrawn from her life, but you, Committee members, you have not kept up your side of the bargain.

I was promised regular updates. However, despite repeated requests, I haven't heard a single word! Inka's fate lies upon my heart as if she was my very own child, and I therefore turn to you again with a question and a request: Where is she now? Is she in the children's home or a private home? If she is in a private home, what are the circumstances? Is she attending school, and if so, a Hebrew school or a Polish school? Does she look well? How is her health, and did she have that operation on her nose?[7] Any details are very important to me.

Please don't think that I would try to come see her – I won't. I care about her peace of mind and would not want to disrupt that.

Just one more question: Does she know the truth about her origins yet? If so, how did she take the news, and has she adjusted to it? Does she remember the past and us? From my side, I pray to God that she should adjust to her new situation as quickly as possible and that it should be as good as possible for her among her own people. I would also ask that you send me a photo of her. Your secretary had promised to send me such a photo, but the matter ended with the promise.

I hope that this letter will not remain unanswered and that I will receive the information I need and which, by moral right, I deserve.

With the appropriate degree of respect,

N. Roztropowicz

I had no idea at that time what was truly happening.

---

7   The surgery was to remove a polyp from Inka's nose. [SH]

CHAPTER 11

Ina Goszczewski

After a few months, in late 1948 or early 1949, a physician who worked at the orphanage, Dr. Sophia (Zosia) Kagan-Goszczewski, approached me and started to shower me with attention. Dr. Goszczewska, as everybody called her, was in her early forties. She had beautiful blonde hair pulled back and held down with pins, blue eyes and a lovely complexion. She always smelled really good. She wore a doctor's white smock, which made her look very pretty. I wondered why she spent so much time with me.

My question was answered when Sophia approached me. She took me aside and said softly, "You must know by now that you are very special to me. I love you very much. Do you have any idea why? It's because I am your mother. I had to leave you when you were a baby with a Polish family to save your life during the war."

Looking at me and touching my shoulders gently, she said, "I want to take you home with me where you belong, so we can be a family again."

I don't think I fully understood what that really meant. In a strange way I resented being singled out for a special treatment. I did not understand how this was going to change my life. I was just beginning to adjust to the life in the orphanage. I wanted to be like the rest of the children and stay there.

The following Monday, I left the orphanage with my new parents. I was going through a metamorphosis one more time. My name and identity would change – I would become Ina Goszczewski.

I walked up the stairs to my new home holding my new mother's hand.

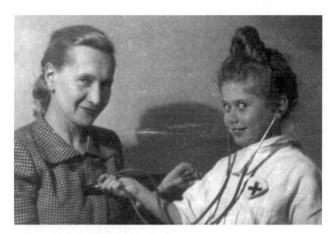

Inka with Sophia Goszczewski, "The Two Doctors," 1949

She rang the doorbell. A man opened the door. This was the first time I saw Zygmund Goszczewski. He was my new dad. I liked him right away – he was tall and handsome. Dad showed me in.

My new home was a spacious apartment. They showed me my room. I had never had my own room before. From my room, they walked me to the dining room.

I remember the furniture in particular. The table, chairs and the break-front seemed huge to me. It seemed like a good place to play hide and seek. A long dark hallway led to the kitchen. At the very end of the hallway was my mother's clinic.

My favorite room became the room between the kitchen and the dining room. Nobody ever sat there. I discovered something there I had never seen before – a record player. The room became my playroom.

There, for the first time, I listened to Beethoven and I loved it. I listened to his music over and over again. I would read there, and let my childish imagination take me to faraway places.

In a very short time, I was transformed from an orphan to a little princess, an only child of doting Jewish parents. I received a new wardrobe and went to a private Jewish school. I started to learn Hebrew and how to form the Hebrew letters, a strange alphabet that reads from right to left. Alma, our maid, used to walk me to school and back.

At home though, I discovered that Sophia was nervous and had a short temper. One day I was curious to see what was happening in the yard of our building, I bent down and looked through the open window. She grabbed me and yelled at me at the top of her lungs about how dangerous that was. This was just a couple of days after I arrived in their house. I was terrified. I burst out crying and sobbed uncontrollably. Only when Dad took me out of the house for a walk did I finally calm down.

His blue eyes were kind and gentle. He spoke softly, and patiently answered all my many questions. I trusted my father completely. He spent time with me. He loved me. He took me to see his store. He was in the textile industry for which Lodz was famous. He was well liked by all; everyone liked him for his sense of humor and fascinating anecdotes. He was a natural storyteller. I noticed that he always wore long sleeved shirts, even on a hot day. I wondered why.

One day he rolled up his sleeve and showed me his hand. I was stunned when I saw the deformity. He told me how it had happened.

"As a young boy, I had an accident. While helping my mother with the laundry, my right hand got caught in the clothes wringer. It was seriously injured. I was taken to Germany for corrective surgery. They saved my hand, but left it deformed. I had to relearn all my daily activities with my left hand."

He was not bitter or angry about what happened to him. He was an eternal optimist. Whenever I was sad or upset, Dad always would know how to cheer me up.

One Shabbat afternoon, we were sitting leisurely and chatting in the kitchen. Dad was in a good mood. It was the right time to ask him the question that had been on my mind for a long time.

"Dad, how did you survive the war? How did you conceal your hand?"

My father's answer was in the form of a short story. "I had a strong physique, and I looked very healthy. When I arrived at the death camp, I instantly understood that the state of my hand could send me to the gas chamber. If the Germans decided to label me disabled, I would immediately be considered useless and destined to death. I managed to conceal my hand by wearing long sleeves. My friends always stood close to me to help cover my hand during the roll call at the concentration camp."

My father added a second reason for his survival – his "job assignment. The Germans put me in charge of the kitchen. Immediately I discovered the importance of being fair and honest with the workers." Before he took over the job, the workers had been stealing food. As a result, some of the prisoners went hungry, or got smaller portions than they were entitled to. When he took over, he changed that. "I talked to the kitchen workers, and proposed that we first feed the prisoners, and whatever was left would be distributed equally among us. Being close to food meant having more strength to survive!"

"Dad, how did you and Mom meet?" I asked curiously

"We met in the Lodz ghetto during the war. We fell in love and got married there."

I was not satisfied with this short statement. I pressured him to tell the entire story. My father told me that he had been married with a daughter. He and Sophia met after a raid on the ghetto in 1942 in which his family was caught by the Germans and put on the train to Auschwitz. "I never saw my wife or daughter again." He was very distraught and stopped reporting for work. He did not eat or sleep and lost the will to live. He contracted a bad cold, which, untreated, turned into pneumonia. "I started to cough blood. I was not productive anymore in the eyes of the Nazis. My friends were worried about my condition."

"One day I woke up and found myself in the hospital. I had no idea how I had gotten there. All I remember was that when I opened my eyes, a young, blonde woman with beautiful blue eyes was standing next to my bed. I assumed she was a doctor because she wore a white smock and had a stethoscope hanging around her neck. She introduced herself as Dr. Kagan, my physician.

"We were hoping you would pull out of the bad pneumonia, and I am thrilled that you did. When you were brought here you were very sick. Don't worry; we will take good care of you."

He was ambivalent about being back among the living. "What for? What was waiting for me out there? The people I loved were gone. Who knew whether I would ever see them again? I didn't care whether I lived or died.

"But Dr. Kagan didn't give up on me so easily. True to her reputation as a dedicated and caring doctor, she made sure I got whatever support I needed, medical or emotional, in order to recover.

"I found myself looking forward to her brief visits. With time, the visits became longer. We talked about everything. At the end of the second week, I was discharged."

At first, Sophia called to see how he was doing health-wise. The attraction was mutual, and they started to see each other regularly and soon became a couple.

"I would not be here today if it wasn't for your mother. She saved my life!"

As horrible as life was in the ghetto, with people dropping dead like flies, they did not know that the worst was yet to come. That day arrived sooner than they expected – the final liquidation of the ghetto. The ghetto was completely evacuated, and all the Jews were deported to concentration camps. They were separated and did not know of each other's fate until after the war.

"We both went through hell. Your mother walked in the death marches. Thousands of people died along the way. Beautiful landscapes bring back bad memories – she saw the most breathtaking sights of nature while her friends dropped dead around her.

"After the war, we started to look for each other. The Jewish community set up a board on which every survivor would write his name, and that was how we eventually found each other."

Everyone spoiled me during the first months at my parents' home in Lodz. My new parents pampered me. Their friends, all Holocaust survivors, made me the center of attention, and of course I loved it.

I also discovered that Sophia was revered and respected by everyone. Among her friends she was somewhat of a legend. I did not really know why.

Since they all were together in the ghetto and the camps, survival stories were a constant topic in our house. I loved staying up late, sitting with the adults and listening to their fascinating stories. It was when we were sitting around the dinner table that Franka, one of my mother's friends, described a scene that took place during a "meal" in their concentration camp. The Jewish inmates stood in a long line for soup. The *Kapo* (the woman in charge of a barrack) was rushing the inmates to move faster. Mom did not move fast enough for the *Kapo* after getting her soup. The *Kapo* struck my mother over the head.

Most women would have reacted by holding their head and screaming in pain. My mother stood still and looked the *Kapo* in the eyes, defiantly spilling the soup on the floor. From that day on, the *Kapo* had a great respect for my mother and never bothered her again.

Another friend of my parents described how my mother had saved his life. He and other prisoners were digging ditches in the fields. It was the harsh, cold winter. Little food and hard work were taking their toll on him, and he was losing his strength. One morning he felt he just could not get up; he was too weak to go to work. My mother heard about this. She brought him to the infirmary and admitted him for a few days of rest. She gave him her daily food ration, her potato. A little rest and some food helped him regain his strength and survive until they were liberated. This same man was having dinner at our home in Lodz when he told us his story.

My mother also talked about her constant dilemma of whether or not to admit a sick person to the clinic, because the Nazis would often pay sudden visits to the clinic and send all the patients to the gas chambers. Sometimes people had a better chance of survival by *not* being put in the infirmary. It was impossible to know what the best thing was to do. So often, just plain luck determined whether a person was going to live or die.[8]

Sophia Kagan-Goszczewski, sixth from left, Lodz ghetto, 1941–1942.

8   My mother was in several camps during the Holocaust, including Auschwitz I believe, but I do not know all the details. [SH]

CHAPTER 12

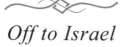

Off to Israel

On November 29, 1947, the United Nations General Assembly voted to partition Mandatory Palestine into a Jewish state and an Arab state. Immediately, the surrounding Arab countries attacked the as yet unformed tiny Jewish state. This became known as Israel's War of Independence. The Arabs were confident they would win the war easily. Even though the Jews were outnumbered – it was David against Goliath once more – the Jews won the war.

Israel became a haven for every oppressed Jew in the world. Jews from all over, just like us, began to arrive in the newly established state. Many thousands had been emigrating to Palestine even earlier, in the "illegal" immigration when the British still controlled the country.

At the end of 1949, my parents informed me that we would be traveling to the new country of Israel. We would be taking the train from Poland to Naples, Italy, and from there we would travel by ship to Haifa, Israel.

We left Lodz at the beginning of January 1950. Although the trip took only a few days, to a child it seemed like an eternity. Conditions on the ship were tough. Our ship was not a luxury liner. We were all seasick. The Mediterranean Sea is stormy in the winter months. The ship's chefs served Italian dishes like crab that the Polish Jews knew were not kosher, and were foreign to their taste. I vaguely remember some men eating garlic bread and the smell of garlic was everywhere!

Otherwise, I don't remember too many details. I guess so many things had happened to me in such a short time that they became suppressed in my memory. I do recall many passengers wiping their tear-stained faces when we approached Haifa. I did not know why they were crying.

I do comprehend it now. They understood the importance of that moment. After 2,000 years in the Diaspora, Jews were going back to their historic homeland. Survivors from the ashes of the Holocaust had lived to witness this miracle. After a long journey they were finally home.

They were anxious to leave behind the memories of the family members who had perished, to erase the appalling violence and murder they had witnessed. There was an exhilarating feeling of a new beginning, of pioneers coming to build a new land. Nothing could deter them. The worst was behind them; the best was yet to come.

Haifa – 1950

It was January 1950. Our Italian ship docked in Haifa, and the three of us descended the gangplank. My father carried our only possessions: one small suitcase and a container of jam. When we reached the ground, we saw an improvised refugee processing area. A smiling government official welcomed us and directed us to the next stop on our journey, a folding table with a stack of documents piled high next to an unfinished sandwich. The methodical clerk dutifully handed a document to Dad. He looked at it and then showed it to Mom.

They carefully examined the document, which was written in Hebrew. It was our new identity card. Then I saw Dad wiping tears streaming down his cheeks. Dad turned to us and said proudly, "We just became the proud citizens of the State of Israel!" I watched my parents laugh and cry simultaneously while I stood there bewildered.

From there, we saw a number of buses waiting in the parking lot. We boarded a bus marked "Tzrifin" (Sarafend), the name of the compound in which we were going to live. Tzrifin was a *maabara*, one of several tent cities in which newcomers were placed while they looked for more permanent housing.

This was the Ellis Island of Israel. All newcomers were taken there straight from the ship. They sometimes lived in a *maabara* for months until the administration found appropriate housing and work for them. Hebrew language classes (*ulpan*) were offered to the newcomers. Government officials were available to help provide the newcomers with whatever assistance necessary.

January is a winter month in Israel. It was rainy and cold, but it did not dampen our high spirits. We walked around trying to get acquainted with our new surroundings. At last our guide stopped and showed us a large tent. He explained that this would be our home until a more permanent arrangement could be found.

I thought that was neat. Sleeping in a tent sounded like an exciting camping trip. I slept very well that first night, awakened only by thunder. I watched Mom put a bucket in the middle of the tent to collect the rainwater coming through the hole.

We were facing a life that all newcomers to Israel did at that time. Israel had to absorb hundreds of thousands of Jewish refugees. It was an enormous task for a poor, new country.

After a week in the *maabara*, my parents were notified that someone was looking for them. All three of us went to the center of the compound, where an elderly gentleman with glasses and silver gray hair was standing. When he saw us, he waved cheerfully and with a smile introduced himself. "I am Nehemiah Rabin, the husband of Rosa Cohen!"

Turning to my mother he said "Rosa, my dear wife – your aunt – passed away very young. She talked about you frequently. We followed the events in Europe with great concern. We worried about your fate, praying you'd survive. I wish my dearest Rosa was here to see that you survived and to greet you in person. I know she would have wanted me to come here and invite you to stay with me in my apartment until you find your own place."

Rosa had died in 1937 from lung cancer, leaving Nehemiah a widower with two children. Their daughter Rachel was now married, living on a kibbutz, and their son Yitzhak was a young officer in the Israel Defense Forces. He would later become IDF Chief of Staff and then Prime Minister of Israel.

My mother knew she had relatives in Israel, but she had never met Nehemiah in person. And now Nehemiah was inviting us to stay in his apartment in Tel Aviv, without really knowing us. We were moved to tears. We were overwhelmed by his kindness. He proudly showed us his shiny blue truck. We did not need much time to decide and ran to our tent to pick up our few belongings. Moments later, we were speeding to our new address, 32 Trumpeldor Street, Tel Aviv. The roads were empty, as not many people owned cars at that time.

CHAPTER 13

Tel Aviv

I will never forget entering Nehemiah's home! Coming from a tent tenement, I thought this was like a palace. A refrigerator stood in the hallway. It was the first *electric* refrigerator I had ever seen. What most people had at that time was an icebox – literally a box with a compartment for storing a large block of ice to keep the food cold. Nehemiah was very proud of his appliance. In the hot Middle Eastern climate it was a basic necessity, but to me it was a luxury.

This apartment was on the second floor of a four-story building that did not have an elevator. For me, that did not pose any problem. I loved sliding down the banisters and running up the stairs, skipping four steps at a time.

It was a two-bedroom apartment. Nehemiah explained that we could use one room, and he would use the other. In addition, there was a tiny kitchen with just enough room for a table and three chairs. The kitchen had a little balcony with a view of the neighboring apartments. We never forgot Nehemiah's great generosity, taking us in and sharing the little he had with us.

Israel was a poor, young country, struggling to survive. Living conditions were difficult and food was rationed. There were shortages of food and housing, but there was a feeling of unity, solidarity and pride. The pioneers were Jews from Russia and Poland primarily. They were very proud of being farmers and working their own land, unlike the Jews in Czarist Russia who were forbidden from owning any land. The working class was considered the aristocracy of Israel. Nehemiah Rabin, who was working at the Electric Company, definitely fell into that category.

We settled down into a routine. Mom, being a doctor, got a job in Kupat Holim, the main health care organization. Dad started working at a textile store belonging to Mom's relatives, the Rutenbergs.

Dad was considered lucky to get a job right away, but he did not see it that way. In Lodz he had had his own business, and now he found himself in the position of an employee, not making the decisions and having to follow orders. He resented it, and was very unhappy. He couldn't wait to open his own shop.

After consulting with Nehemiah, my parents made a decision regarding my schooling. Nehemiah insisted I enroll at Beit Hinukh, a local socialist elementary school that his wife Rosa had helped establish. The students were children of pioneers and workers, the elite element of Israeli society in the 1950s. There were two sessions: one in the morning and another in the afternoon. Mine started at 1 pm.

My first school day in Israel was a painful experience. Nehemiah took me to school, introducing me to the principal as his cousin. Then, I met my new second grade teacher, Leah. (We called the teachers by their first names.) She put her arm around my shoulder and took me into the classroom. She introduced me to the class and asked me to sit down at the first desk, right in the front of the class. Leah felt this might ease my adjustment to my new surroundings.

She was wrong. I sat there not understanding what was going on behind my back. I was in a daze. Things were happening too fast. I could feel the other children staring at me, whispering to each other and giggling. I knew they were making jokes about me. They were mimicking my strong Polish "r" and imitating the way I pronounced the few words I knew in Hebrew. They were pointing to my strange hairstyle and my fancy dresses. I sat there for hours unable to communicate with anyone.

At recess, things got even worse. It was a full-blown circus, and I was the butt of their ridicule. The boys did not bother me much, as they were busy playing ball. The girls, however, were a different story. Esther was their leader. She was the embodiment of a *sabra* – olive skin, big brown eyes, and beautiful curly hair. She was giggly and funny as well as petite and skinny. She also could outrun every other student in the class. Whatever she said or did, everyone followed.

Esther approached me and motioned at me with her finger to join them in a game. It was hide and seek. She showed me how to cover my eyes and count to ten. I did. When I opened my eyes they were all gone. Since I was new and did not know the schoolyard as well as they did I ended up running and looking for them until the bell rang and we went back to class. On the way, I heard them laughing at my futile efforts to find them.

Even though I had been exposed to the Hebrew alphabet in Poland, it was different now. Here in Israel, Hebrew was the language used in daily life, not just for studying in school. The sound of the Hebrew language was harsh and foreign to me. It sounded different from anything I had ever heard before.

I faced an alphabet that went from right to left. I was confused at first, as to what side of the notebook to start writing. There were letters and then there were dots under the letters. I realized later they were the vowels. I was hopelessly frustrated and discouraged.

Since I was the oldest, I was the tallest in my class. This made me even more self–conscious. It did not go unnoticed by Esther. After school she put on a little show for everyone. She walked behind me pretending to be me, looking like some awkward clumsy giant trotting along heavily.

At last Esther confronted me and said, "How old are you, Inka?"

"Eight," I answered innocently, unaware of what would follow.

Esther blurted loudly, "I knew it! You were retained! Big and dumb!" The other children echoed her, chanting, "Big and dumb, big and dumb!"

I ran all the way home without looking back. I leapt up the stairs without stopping, entering the apartment like a storm. I jumped onto my bed and cried and cried until I fell asleep. I hated the children, the school, the teacher, and the horrible language she was forcing me to learn. My life was a living hell.

The children did not look kindly on my appearance. My hair was styled according to the latest Polish hairstyle – I had a big lock on top of my head, and in the back two ponytails were tied by delicate white and pink silk ribbons. My sheer white blouse and plaid skirt were much too elegant for this school. Israeli fashion then was very plain and unisex: khaki shorts and shirt, or denim overalls, for both boys and girls.

I was the laughing stock of my class.

I knew what I had to do. I devoted all my energies to making the necessary changes in order to fit in. I changed my hairstyle, got new clothes and worked on my accent. I wanted to look and sound like a *sabra*.

One February evening, I was doing my homework at my desk in our family's room. Dad was sitting in a corner reading the newspaper. Nehemiah was smoking his pipe in his room listening to the latest news on the radio when the doorbell rang. It was Rachel, Nehemiah's daughter.

We had been waiting for her all evening, so we all ran to the door to greet her. We had been expecting her to arrive earlier, as supper was already on the table.

She apologized for being late; the bus from Kiryat Shemona arrived late. She was exhausted from the five-and-a-half hour bus ride and the heat. She walked into Nehemiah's room and gave her dad a kiss on the cheek.

Rachel was slim and medium-built; she usually wore simple white cotton blouses and dark skirts, sometimes with embroidery at the bottom. Her brown wavy hair was always tied in a thick beautiful braid. She never wore any makeup. She was a typical kibbutz member: modest, hard working and very patriotic. She was always full of energy, but talked slowly, measuring every word. Rachel and her brother Yitzhak had an identical voice, slow and clear, unmistakably "Rabin-unique."

We sat down to eat and Rachel turned to me and asked, "So, how is school, Inka? Is your Hebrew improving?"

"The kids in school are mean! They make fun of my accent. They gang up on me. Half of the time I don't understand what the teacher is saying in Hebrew!"

I complained passionately. The only reason I stopped was because Mom looked annoyed listening to me.

Rachel felt sorry for me, but she out loud she said, "It's only a matter of time before your friends discover what a nice person you really are. They will love you."

"I doubt I will ever like them after the way they're treating me now!" I said with tears in my eyes.

Mom interrupted our conversation. "Inka, did you finish your dinner? It's time to go to bed. Don't worry! Everything will be ok!"

Dad went back to reading his newspaper. Rachel and Mom went to do the dishes in the kitchen and I went to bed. I could hear them whispering in the kitchen, but I could barely make out what they were saying. From what Rachel disclosed years later, I believe their conversation went something like this. Rachel asked Mom, "Did you tell Inka what exactly happened to her during the war?"

"I told her she is Jewish and that she is our daughter. I explained how we left her with the Roztropowicz family when the ghetto was liquidated. When the war ended, we looked for her everywhere and eventually found her in the orphanage."

"Did Inka believe your story?"

"Yes. She seemed to accept it."

"Does Inka talk about the Roztropowicz family? Does it look like she misses them?"

"No, she never mentions them. It seems she has forgotten them. She does not talk about the past. I strongly feel it is better for her to forget the horrible way her young life started."

"Are you going to tell Inka about the adoption?"

Mom became very agitated at Rachel's question. This time she raised her voice and said very firmly, "Absolutely not! Never!"

Rachel was not moved. She persisted with her questioning. "What if one of your friends mentions it to her? Aren't you better off telling her yourself?"

"My friends all are aware of my decision, and I know they will all stand by me. They are not going to betray me, and neither are you! I know what is best for Inka! It is best she forgets her past." Then she added in a low voice, "We want to start a new chapter in our lives."

Rachel decided to drop the subject for the time being. She then went to her purse and pulled out some food stamps. "You will need these when you go shopping at the grocery store."

Mom thanked Rachel and added, "It is essential that Inka gets the best nutrition possible. She had tuberculosis during the war and suffered from malnutrition. We can do without, but she must eat well."

Rachel nodded her head in agreement.

CHAPTER 14

Friends

The morning began just like any other. Nehemiah was out doing errands. Dad had left for work. Mom came over to where I was eating breakfast and said sternly: "Inka, don't forget to sweep the floor and dust the furniture. After all, we are guests in Nehemiah's apartment! We need to keep the place clean! When you are done cleaning, do your homework. I will be home at around 12 to make lunch and take you to school!"

As soon as she closed the door, I took the remainder of my breakfast and threw it over the balcony, down to the yard where it splattered on the ground. I joyfully watched the birds devour it within a few seconds.

Then I called from our balcony to my friend Aviva on the ground floor, "Aviva, ask your mom if I can come downstairs to play!" Aviva was an older neighborhood girl, who unfortunately did not attend the same school I did.

I ran back onto the kitchen balcony when I heard Aviva's voice calling me, "Inka, you can come down. My mom said it's ok."

Happily, I slammed our apartment door behind me, never bothering to lock the door. I slid down the stairway's wide wooden banister. This was faster, and a lot of fun.

Aviva and I managed to communicate despite my limited Hebrew. We played and enjoyed ourselves immensely. Aviva's mother made me feel welcome by offering me a snack. I was having the time of my life. Aviva was older than me and she was nice to me. She actually liked me, not like the kids in school who kept teasing me and laughing at me. I wanted to stay in Aviva's house forever!

Suddenly Aviva's mom came into the room where we were playing, visibly upset. She turned to me and said "Inka, your mother is looking for you everywhere. She does not know where you are. You better run home and let her know you are here."

I dropped everything and ran up the stairs as fast as I could, skipping two steps at a time. As I entered the apartment, my mother greeted me with a roaring voice.

"Where were you?!" Not waiting for an answer, she continued to scream, "I told you to stay here and do your work! Did you do what you were supposed to do? Answer me!"

She grabbed me, holding me by the hand forcefully and demanding an answer in a menacing way. I was scared. I decided to lie. "Yes, I did."

My mother's face turned white, her thin lips lost all color, and her eyes narrowed as if she had been struck by lightning. Before I knew what was happening, she dragged me by my hair to the wall and started to bang my head against the wall over and over again, all the time yelling, "Never lie to me again! I can't stand liars!"

After what seemed as an eternity, she finally let go. I was so shaken I could not even cry. I instinctively straightened my hair. I ran into the bathroom and slammed the door behind me. I sat on the toilet seat and finally started to sob. Then I washed my face with cold water, worrying what the kids would think when they saw my red eyes.

When I returned to the kitchen, I saw that my mother had prepared lunch. I could not eat. Irritated, my mother snapped, "Aren't you going to eat anything?"

I shook my head, unable to say anything. Then Mom urged me to hurry up and get ready for school because she had to return to work in the clinic.

I walked to school with her. We didn't talk. I felt so sad and empty inside.

I don't think Dad ever found out what happened to me in our house that morning. I never told him because I felt that he would not do anything about it anyway. What I did not understand then was that Dad was in some ways dependent on Mom. He was handicapped, and she took care of him. Above all, she had that aura of a living legend in the Polish community for her heroism during the Holocaust. As a child I felt so helpless, with no one to be my advocate. The fears of not being loved and of being abandoned that had lain dormant returned. They were always present, just below the surface.

The following day at school, something good happened. A freckle-faced redhead girl named Mira approached me at recess. I didn't know what to expect, so I just stood there, waiting to see what she wanted. She asked, "Where do you live?"

I replied, "On Trumpeldor Street, across from the old cemetery. We live with my mom's cousin, Nehemiah Rabin."

Mira then asked, "Do you want to be my friend? My mom said we can walk to school together, since we are almost neighbors. Would you like that? My mom told me about your cousin. He is an important person. Everybody likes him."

I was so excited about Mira's offer of friendship that I didn't hear what else she said. After all Mira was a *sabra*, well liked by all my classmates. I was flattered that she liked me enough to want to be my friend.

I answered without hesitation, "Yes, of course! Let's be friends and walk to school together."

That day after school, I skipped all the way home! Things were looking up for me! I had a friend! Mira and I became close friends. We walked to and from school together every day.

On the way home from school one day, Mira said, "Inka, do you want to come to my house? We can do our homework and then play, and you can eat supper with my family." That was the first time anybody from school had invited me to their home.

"Yes! Yes! That will be so much fun!" I said.

The next day, instead of going home and waiting for my mother to return from the clinic, I walked with Mira to her house. Mira's mother was home. She was expecting us. She had prepared some cookies and milk. The cookies were still warm from the oven.

I stared with amazement at their oven. We didn't have an oven; we only had gas burners. My mother did not spend much time in the kitchen.

We did our homework together. Mira and I gossiped about children at school while we played ball with other children who lived on her street. Around 7 pm, Mira's mom called us into the house for supper.

We washed our hands and faces and entered the kitchen. Mira's father,

brother and mother were sitting around the table, on which were a big vegetable salad, a basket of bread, some butter and cheeses. We helped ourselves
to the fresh delicious food while talking and laughing.

We had a great time. It was nice to have a big family, and a mother who
stayed home and was relaxed and smiling.

After dinner, Mira's father said, "It's getting late. We better take Inka
home." Mira and her father walked me home. We said goodnight in front of
my apartment building, and I ran upstairs.

When I entered our apartment that night, it seemed dark, quiet and
gloomy in comparison to Mira's. My mother seemed so tired from working
hard at the clinic all day. She was sitting in the kitchen, reading the newspaper
and eating jam out of a jar. Dad was in our room listening to the news on the
radio. As I looked at my parents, I realized that each of them was doing their
own thing. Were we a family?

I talked to Mira about my loneliness. "Are your parents home in the
afternoons? Do you always eat dinner together with your family?"

The answer was always *yes*. I asked myself why I couldn't have a normal family like hers.

After several very long months in second grade, I began to look forward
to summer vacation. But before things got better, they got worse.

My mother delivered the bad news to me during supper. "Inka, this may
not sound like good news to you, but we feel that this will help you in school.
We hired a private tutor to teach you Hebrew during the summer. Right now
you are the oldest student in your class. When you pass the test at the end of
summer you will go straight to fourth grade, skipping third."

My heart sank when I heard this. My parents could see the pain in my
eyes. They comforted me, promising to take me on a trip to Kibbutz Manara,
where Rachel and her family lived. I remember that summer as the longest
one I ever experienced. I don't remember my tutor, but I do remember how I
hated studying Hebrew.

At the end of August, just as my parents had promised, they put me on
the bus to the town of Kiryat Shmona, a short drive from Manara. Even though
it was a five-and-a-half-hour journey, I didn't mind. Rachel and her husband
Rafi picked me up and took me to Manara.

I knew I had to be on my best behavior, for many reasons. Rachel was,
after all Nehemiah's daughter, and we owed Nehemiah so much. She was also

a teacher, and had high standards. She was a person of principles and high moral values. To tell the truth, I didn't know if I could live up to her standards. It made me feel uneasy.

My behavior was guarded all the time, whether at home with Mom or with Nehemiah. Dad was the only one with whom I could really be myself. He accepted me the way I was. In his eyes I could do no wrong. Only a stern look would let me know when he was not pleased with me.

I enjoyed Manara because it was so different from my life in Tel Aviv. Manara is located on top of a mountain. I loved to go and sit on the cliff behind the cultural center, and look out over the green northern Galilee valley below, which was once swampland. In the morning Rafi would show me the chicken coop with hundreds of chickens, and the barn where they milked the cows using the latest technology. We would walk by the nursery and the building where the children lived separately from their parents. Every day at 5p.m., Tirza, Yiftah and Gadi – Rachel and Rafi's three children – would come to their parents' apartment for tea and cake. It was family time.

On the day I was to return home, Rachel's brother Yitzhak and his wife Leah came for a visit to Manara. We all went to a scenic area with a fantastic view of the Galilee. We sat and talked. Yitzhak was somewhat kind shy and not very talkative; Leah was friendly and bubbly. I remember Yitzhak being concerned about his English. They were about to go to the Staff College, Camberley, in Surrey, England for a year. Leah promised to help him and begged him not to worry.

I was happy they came because it meant I did not have to take the bus home; they were going to take me in Yitzhak's military car. I had lots of fun. Still, at the end of my visit in Manara, I was happy to go home.

CHAPTER 15

Our Own Place

I must have been the only child in Israel that was happy that summer was over and school had started.

Mom had been working temporarily at a *Kupat Holim* clinic close to Nehemiah's apartment. A few months later, she got a permanent position in a different clinic. The down side was that it was far away from our home. She had to take two buses each way. At noon she would return home to prepare dinner. Between 1 and 4 pm, all businesses were closed. They reopened at 4:00. So at about 3:30 pm Mom would have to go back to work. No wonder she was always stressed out.

My parents were anxious to get their own place. They felt we were imposing on Nehemiah, even though he was a gracious host. About a year after our arrival, we moved to our own apartment – 11 Bikurei Hitim Street, in Tel Aviv. Although we were ecstatic to finally have our own home, I was sad to leave my friend Aviva behind. While we were still in the same city, the new apartment was more than a mile away. Since neither of our parents drove, I knew I would not see her anymore.

Our new home was in one of four apartment buildings in a new housing development. It had two rooms and a hallway, a balcony facing the backyard, and a tiny square kitchen with just enough room for a refrigerator, a small table and two stools. A third stool stood half in the kitchen and half in the hallway.

One day, Mom returned home unusually early. When the three of us sat down to eat supper, she said to Dad and me, "I have a surprise! Yesterday I ran into a young woman called Erna. I know her from the time I worked at the orphanage in Lodz. Her parents perished in the Holocaust."

Mom got up to boil some water for tea. When she returned to the table, she continued, "When I first saw her at the orphanage, she immediately reminded me of my brother Izio's girlfriend, Justina. Izio and Justina died during the Holocaust. I lost contact with Erna when we left for Israel. I had no idea that she came to Israel too, and lives in Tel Aviv. We talked for a long time. She told me what has happened to her since I last saw her in Lodz. She's sick – she has a severe case of ulcers with no one to care for her. Right now she is staying in a woman's shelter. We need to help her. So I offered to let her move in with us until she feels better and gets back on her feet. What do think, Inka? You will have to share your room with her."

I didn't mind. At nineteen, Erna was older than I, but much younger than my parents! I liked the idea of having another young person in the house. I jumped up and down with excitement. This was great news!

The next day, I got up very early. The truth is, I could hardly sleep, thinking about Erna. We had to get ready for her. Mom emptied the closet, and made room for Erna's clothes. I cleaned my room and bought some fresh cut flowers to welcome her. I bombarded my mother with questions about Erna, but Mom only answered, "She will be here tomorrow. You can ask her yourself. I think you are going to like her."

Erna arrived on Friday, just as I returned from school. She was tall, skinny and pale. When she approached to give me a hug and a kiss, I could see how beautiful she was. She had blue eyes and a short haircut. Erna had a lovely smile, and when she laughed, you could see the dimples in both cheeks.

Mom asked, "Inka, why don't you show Erna the room and the closet that you two will share?" I did so enthusiastically.

Erna was anxious to become part of the family. She offered to help in the kitchen and do other chores around the house. She was well aware of my mother's busy schedule.

At night, when we were supposedly getting ready to go to sleep, Erna and I would talk. She would tell me some of what she went through during the war, and how she managed to survive. Whispering so Mom wouldn't hear, Erna described her life.

"I lived with my family in Warsaw. Then, the Nazis separated us from the rest of the Poles by putting us in one small area and surrounding it with a high wall. That was the ghetto. We suffered terribly. We had hardly any food. The winter was unbearable, and we endured the freezing cold without heat. One night, we heard the sound of loud pounding on the door and a voice yelling, 'Police! Open up!'

"As my mom opened the door, four Nazis barged in. They dragged my dad with them and disappeared into the night. That was the last time I saw him.

"After that, Mom decided to get me out of the ghetto. Our Polish housekeeper was the only outside connection we had. On Thursday, after dinner, Mom said she needed to talk to me. She had tears in her eyes when she hugged me and whispered, 'Whatever happens, don't forget where you came from. Above all, remember that I love you, and I did this so you will live.'

"That night they took me to the wall surrounding the ghetto. After bribing the guard, they pushed me over to the Aryan side of Warsaw. There I met the family that took me in. That was the last time I saw my Mom. She perished with the rest of the Jews deported from the Warsaw ghetto. It marked a further descent into my personal hell."

I could see how Erna was reliving all her experiences. So I gently said, "Maybe we should call it a night?"

Erna replied, "Yes, I am tired. Good night!"

Then I whispered, "Do you want to be my sister?"

Erna said dozing off, "Yes. We'll always be sisters!"

I was so happy! I was not alone. Erna was with me. She helped me with the house chores. At nineteen, she dated a lot. I helped her decide what to wear for a date. She showed me how to put on make up. We had private jokes that only the two of us understood.

I would wait for her at night to hear about her recent date. We discussed the guys at length. We would whisper and giggle half of the night.

Erna's relationship with my mom was a different story. The two of them clashed often. Sometimes I saw Erna cry. Finally, Erna decided she wanted a place of her own.

I was shocked when Erna announced she was leaving. It was such a blow. I refused to accept the new situation. I was grief-stricken. I hated change. People I loved always seemed to leave me.

I felt sad and abandoned once more.

Because my parents were spending so much time working, it was decided that we would hire a housekeeper. After inquiring among our friends, we found Tamara, who seemed to relate well to all the members of the family. In addition to the housework, Tamara also did the shopping, and cooked the family meals. Although she only was there for a few hours each day, she became part of the family. She ended up being with us for nearly two-and-a-half years.

I stayed at the same school, but I also made friends in the new neighborhood. They treated me as their equal. Now that I could communicate in Hebrew, school became a little easier. Home life still had its ups and downs, but not as often. I was starting to feel better about myself. No one was teasing me or making fun of me anymore. I was on my way to becoming a *sabra*!

An orchard of oranges grew across the street from our apartment building. My friends loved to play in the orchard. We didn't have fancy games. We used our imagination and played "Hide and Go Seek" and "House."

My mother would bring us broken stethoscopes, bandages and smocks from the medical clinic where she worked. My friends and I would use them when we played "Doctor and Patient." We would go to each other's home; sometimes we ate meals together. We knew all the parents, and all parents knew every child. They all watched over us. It was our own world; there was a strong sense of community. Even though at home I was frequently alone, in the neighborhood, I felt a sense of safety.

On the holiday of *Sukkot,*[9] the children looked for wood and sticks to build a *sukkah*. We put up the frame of the *sukkah* together with the help of some parents, and then we hung blankets to make the walls. We covered the top with palm branches, as was the custom. The greatest fun was decorating the *sukkah* with fruits and vegetables. In the evening, the parents prepared

---

9   Sukkot, the holiday of Tabernacles, commemorates the biblical times when the Israelites lived in temporary huts in the desert following their exodus from Egypt. It is also the Jewish harvest holiday in the Land of Israel.

holiday dishes, the children sang holiday songs and we ate all our meals together in the *sukkah*.

School was now the happier part of my day. On the way home, I often wondered whether somebody was waiting for me, or if I would find an empty house. I was the original latchkey kid.

As I put the key in the lock, my heart would pound, hoping that Tamara would greet me. I knew my parents would not be there. Unfortunately, most of the time, Tamara had left a short time before I arrived. She had a family of her own. I could still smell the aroma of the food she had prepared coming from the kitchen.

I'd warm up the food and eat by myself in the kitchen. Later, I would do my homework. I envied the children who had a mother at home, someone waiting for them with a smile and a hot meal. Sometimes I would walk to a neighbor's apartment and play with a friend.

In the evenings, I would often go out on our balcony. From there, I had a good view of the neighborhood. To my right I could see the Reisman family – father, mother and two daughters sitting together at the kitchen table having supper. In front of me was an elderly couple. I could see their daughter and her children entering their apartment, ready to join them for supper. My feelings of sadness and loneliness resurfaced. Here I was, locked in the darkness again.

When I mentioned some of my frustrations to my father, he would always have the same response. "Inka, you know how much your mother loves you," he would say. "But that's the way she is. You have to accept her the way she is! There is nothing I can do about it. She comes down on me too at times."

On the surface, our family seemed happy. However I did not feel that way. Often I found myself feeling melancholy for no apparent reason. I would not show this side of myself when others were around, only when I was alone. I would fantasize about what life would be like if my family were more cheerful and spent more time together like the Reisman family.

One night around the dinner table, my mother's best friend, Felka Olszer, said to her, "Sophia, why don't you let Inka do some of the house chores? She's a big girl now. Let her help you, and then you won't need the cleaning woman!"

Mom turned to Felka and insisted, "Absolutely not! Inka helps only on

Saturdays. She needs to study and play now. She will have plenty of time to clean as an adult."

Felka, who held my mother in high regard, did not pursue the subject. She kept silent.

My parents formed their ideas on parenting as they went along. There was no counseling for Holocaust survivors. Sophia and Zygmund had been thrown into a completely new country and were fighting to survive, day by day. On top of this, every one of us struggled to become a family. Bonding is a process, lengthy at times. Since Sophia and Zygmund were not my biological parents, it was doubly hard for them. They were learning by trial and error – at the time, mostly by error.

There were nights when I would wake up from my sleep to my mother screaming. I heard her complaining loudly to Dad, "Once again Inka didn't put the dishes in the right place. I've told her a thousand times how to do it! She forgot to put the meat back in the refrigerator. She forgot to sweep the floor again! That girl is so sloppy! No man will ever want her!"

In bed with my eyes closed, pretending to be asleep, I could hear every word she said. I dreaded these frequent scenes at night. Some of the things she said hurt me very deeply. No matter how hard I tried to please her, she was never satisfied.

I never heard my father say a word. He never uttered a word in my defense. I figured he just kept hiding behind the newspaper, pretending to be reading. He would not confront her, or stand up for me as I wished he would.

Saturday, Shabbat, is a day of rest in Israel. There is hardly any traffic. There is little public transportation. Most stores are closed. Many coffee shops and restaurants are not open. People enjoy getting together with family in their homes.

I anticipated Shabbat with mixed feelings. I looked forward to a day off from school, but at home it was a day of cleaning. My first job was to get all my family's shoes onto the tiny kitchen balcony where I had to shine and polish them for the coming week. When that was done, I had to remove all the mops, pots, pans and dishes from the kitchen. Then I had to clean the kitchen thoroughly and later dust the furniture all over the apartment. I didn't mind the work so much, but often my mother would yell, "Inka! Come and make your bed!"

I did what I was told and then returned to my original chore, when she would call me again, "Inka take out the trash!"

She would make me run like that all morning. I felt like Cinderella.

Since we had no phones in our area (no telephone lines had been laid yet in our neighborhood), friends could not call us to let us know that they would be coming by for a visit. Therefore, on Saturdays, friends of my parents would often drop by without any notice. Mom understandably resented these surprise visits.

"Who can that be? I'm not expecting anybody. Inka, get the door!"

Felka and her family were at the door. I let them in. How I loved Felka, her husband Heniek and their son Ben! She was pretty, calm and cheerful. When I kissed her, I could smell her pleasant perfume. I loved it when friends came over; it would transform our place from solemn and miserable to happy and alive.

Mom was nervous and frantic. While our company was standing in the hallway, she hustled me to the living room where Dad was taking a nap. (The living room doubled as my parents' bedroom at night.) I closed the door behind me. I quickly woke him up and changed the convertible sofa back into a couch. I collected the stuff lying on the floor and carried it to the other room, trying to make the room presentable.

I then opened the door, and invited the Olszers in. I loved listening to their stories, and especially to Dad's jokes. He was always the life of the party.

Even though I would have loved to stay, Mom inevitably called me into the kitchen to help her. Dad stayed with the Olszers. Everyone knew Mom wasn't good in the kitchen. It would take her hours to get a meal ready if I didn't help. Tamara spent the weekends with her own family.

I walked into the kitchen, anxious to speed up the supper preparations so I could return to the fun in the living room. Mom was still irritated by the unexpected visitors, and started to give me orders to do things the way she liked to. As I was preparing the salad, she yelled, "Inka, stand on the chair and get the glasses out of the cupboard, wash them and dry them with a towel! Make sure there are no spots!"

I did as I was told. Mom took the glasses to inspect them. She was not happy. She complained, "I see spots on the glasses! You can't serve tea to company in spotty glasses. Do it again!" I did, and then I went back to preparing the salad.

"Inka go look for a tablecloth." I brought a white tablecloth. "That's the wrong one. Get the white one with the flowers!"

As I was looking for the right tablecloth, I heard Mom calling to me again loudly, so everybody could hear. "Inka, you forgot to take out the plates! How many times do I have to repeat the same thing? You should know by now!"

From the corner of my eye (there was no door to the kitchen), I could see everyone exchanging glances, uncomfortable hearing Mom screaming. I was so humiliated. I ran into my room and refused to leave. I was confused and scared and hurt. I had been sobbing for quite some time when Felka came into the room. She sat down on my bed and hugged me.

I felt safe with her. I confided, "I don't know what is right and what is wrong anymore. I try my best to please my mother, but she is never happy. She is nervous and angry all the time. She lashes out at me at the slightest thing." I burst out crying again, unable to control myself.

Felka held my face gently and said very seriously, "Inka, you have to understand that your mother is an amazing human being. She was so brave during the Holocaust. She saved so many of our friends' lives, people that you and I know. Yet she lost her entire family. That is why she is so miserable. Please understand! Don't ever forget what a hero your mother is! In camps they called her "the angel in white." We all love and admire her. She loves you in her own way! You have to understand."

Mom entered the room. Oblivious to what just happened, she asked, "Inka why are you crying? What's wrong? We are all waiting for you so we can start supper!"

"I'm not hungry. Start eating without me. I'll join you later," was my reply.

Felka and Mom left the room. I didn't care what my mother had or hadn't done during the war. I didn't care what a great doctor she was! Why couldn't I have a calm and loving mother like other kids? I hated her!

I felt sad and neglected. Nobody really cared how I felt. Nobody supported me, even when I was right. I stayed in my dark room that entire hot summer night. They were all enjoying themselves. Dad told his jokes, and they all laughed with delight. Nobody really missed me. I was all alone in the world. I cried and cried until I fell asleep.

My graduation from elementary school was not the happy occasion it was supposed to be. It was marred by one upsetting fact – my grades were low. As a result, I did not get into the best high school, located right across from our apartment. While many of my friends would attend that school, I had to go somewhere else. It was embarrassing.

One night, I overheard my parents whispering my name. They thought I was asleep. I strained to hear what they were saying. They were talking about high school. I guessed that it was important since they did not want me to hear. They knew that my low grades would be an obstacle to getting into a good high school. Mom said "Why don't we send her to a kibbutz? They don't look at grades there."

The kibbutz education system was different than in the cities. Grades were not used to evaluate a student's progress. Things have changed since I was a child, but at that time, at a kibbutz you learned for the sake of learning. There were no formal evaluations – no tests, and therefore no grades. The teachers were not accredited. When you finished at a kibbutz high school, you did not get a diploma, and you could not immediately be accepted into a college or university. Those wishing to enter higher education had to take a special exam.

When Dad reacted to my mother's suggestion in an unusually forceful way, it really surprised me. "No way! My daughter will not go to a kibbutz! She will stay home and continue studying! If necessary, I will send her to a private school!"

Mom replied, "Do you have any idea how expensive this private school might be? Can we afford it?"

"We'll manage!"

This time he prevailed. It was one of the few times my father stood up for me. I loved him for that. I wanted to run and kiss him, but I restrained myself because I had heard something I was not supposed to hear.

CHAPTER 16

High School

Life grew more tranquil at home. We all had our routines, which helped me make the adjustments necessary in high school. Dad had faith in me when nobody else did. I was determined not to disappoint him. I was going to do whatever it took to succeed.

My new high school was a large gray building on Geulah Street close to Allenby Street – a well-known shopping area. The other end of Geulah Street bordered the beach on the Mediterranean Sea. It was a small high school; we stayed in the homeroom with the homeroom teacher all day. Other teachers, for subjects like Math, Biology and English, came to our room. We developed a strong bond with our homeroom teacher and formed many friendships with our classmates.

I remember fondly the honor system our homeroom teacher used when he administered a test. He wanted to instill in us a sense of honesty. Nobody cheated! How could we, when he showed us how much he trusted us?

At high school, I finally got recognition for my hard work. Still, my appearance needed much improvement. I was very conscious of this; looks are everything to a teenager. I hated the school uniform! It consisted of a dark-blue oversized blouse and a dull-looking gray skirt. The skirt was long – way past my knees – and it covered the one beautiful part of my body: my legs. It did not compliment my figure. It made me look heavy. I felt like an ugly duckling.

I enjoyed walking to and from Geulah High School. Every day, I passed by a retirement hotel. One elderly lady used to sit near the fence facing the street. She would smile and wave at me. It made me feel like she cared about me and was waiting to see me.

One afternoon as I was walking with my mother, I noticed a gathering of a few people near the hotel. As we approached the crowd, I saw my friend, the elderly lady from the hotel, lying flat in the middle of the street, with cars swerving around her so as not to hurt her. She was in a fetal position, her mouth covered with white foam. She was moaning and groaning. None of the spectators did anything to help her, though she was obviously in distress.

Mom was enraged. She turned to me and said, "When you see a sick person in need of medical help, you cannot just ignore them, even if it is a stranger! You need to get help immediately!" Mom took the sick lady in a taxi to the nearest hospital and stayed with her until she recovered from her epileptic seizure. It was a lesson I would never forget.

I was so proud of my mother that afternoon! I assumed she had saved a life – not just any life, but my friend's life. Now I understood why Sophia's friends were always praising her. She really was a hero!

The last day of my first year in high school finally arrived. I couldn't wait to show my report card to Mom and Dad. I looked at Dad's expression as he slowly opened the card and saw my grades. I could see the transformation on his face, from concern to a broad smile. He and Mom turned to me and said, "This is an outstanding report card. We are so proud of you!" In the space of one year, I had gone from a C student to an A student!

My emergence as a good student bolstered my self-esteem. I made new friends both in school and in my neighborhood. I no longer felt like a refugee. I felt like any other teenager in Israel. I had a sense of belonging. The Hebrew language was not an obstacle anymore. I had mastered the language and dis-covered I was intelligent.

It was during the summer of my second year in high school that life changed for my family. My mother was taking a continuing education class at Beilinson Hospital in Petah Tikvah, near Tel Aviv. As she was crossing the street to catch the bus home, a motorcycle hit her in a hit-and-run accident. She suffered a concussion and a broken arm and was hospitalized. Eventually she recovered, but she was never the same again. Although my mother had been high-strung, after the accident, her temper flared more frequently, and her sense of time was affected. That in turn changed our family life.

One day after school I went to my mother's clinic for some blood work.

After they took a sample of my blood in the lab, I stopped by her waiting room. She was busy examining a patient, so I sat down on a bench and waited for her with other patients.

An elderly gentleman said to the young woman sitting next to him, "I have been waiting for Dr. Goszczewski for the last three hours. If it wasn't Dr. Goszczewski, I would have changed doctors."

The young woman responded, "I've known Dr. Goszczewski since I was a little girl. She knows my whole family – my grandmother, my parents. She is a wonderful doctor and human being, but her hours are crazy! She comes to work in the afternoon and stays at the clinic until midnight."

The elderly gentleman agreed. "I understand she locks the clinic at night, as all the employees go home around 7 pm. We would complain to the administration if it was anybody else, but it is worth the wait to see Dr. Goszczewski."

The young woman agreed. "Yes, you don't find doctors like her anymore, so devoted to her patients. I wonder how her family feels about her being at work until midnight."

I couldn't help overhearing their conversation. I left in a hurry, before they could discover who I was. But I was disturbed by their conversation. I was pleased to hear what the patients had to say about my mother behind her back. I was proud to know she was such a great doctor. At the same time, however, I was distressed by the criticism. Deep in my heart, I could identify with the patients, but I could not tell them that my mother could no longer wake up early in the morning. She would arise around noon, and get to work only around 2 pm. Sometimes when I was coming home from school I would see her heading for work. I knew these were not her normal work hours, but what could I do?

And yet, there were normal times too, which I remember fondly. On those rare occasions, she would come home early and we'd sit in the kitchen. I would bring my homework and she would help me with my French lessons and writing essays. In 1957, I wrote an essay entitled, "Israel in the Year 2000." I believed that peace would prevail and described how it would change everyone's life in Israel and in the whole region. The year 2000 seemed so far away. As I write this, it is now 2011, and sadly none of my rosy predictions has materialized.

Sometimes she would talk about her life. It was on one such occasion that she told me her life story. For as long as she could remember, she had wanted to be a doctor. She was not able to study in Poland. There was a quota severely limiting the number of Jews that could be admitted to medical school in Poland, so she had to travel to France in 1932 to study medicine.

Sophia was a very courageous person. At that time, it was unheard of for a young Jewish woman to travel to a different country to study medicine. But she did it! She faced many obstacles studying medicine in a foreign country in a new language. On top of that, she also faced financial problems. Her father, who supported her for the first year, could not send her any more money the following year, which meant that she had to get a job to support herself.

However, in order to work in France, every foreigner was required to obtain a work permit. Being on a student visa, she could not get one and was forced to work as a cleaning woman. She had to be tough. She would sleep three or four hours a night after studying, and spend the day in classes or at work. Yet, she overcame all obstacles and became a physician.

She graduated and returned home to Poland, where she had to take all the medical exams again. She started to work at a hospital in Lodz. A couple of years later, war broke out. Doctors were desperately needed to take care of the many people sick with infectious diseases. Her youth and profession saved her life. I thought she was so determined and brave. I didn't think I would ever measure up to her.

On another occasion, Mom surprised me. "I would like to talk to you about an intimate subject," she said. I held my breath, wondering what it was. Then she said bluntly, "I want to talk to you about the facts of life."

She explained the reproductive system of men and women scientifically. Then she added, "When you start dating, Inka I want you to remember that you can always count on me to help you. I don't want you to be afraid to tell me anything. If by any chance you get pregnant, you can always count on me to help you, if necessary – even for an abortion." Nobody worried then about sexually transmitted diseases. The worst that could happen to a girl was to get pregnant.

On those rare occasions that we spent time together, I realized how fortunate I was to have such an intelligent and caring mother who wanted me to know that she would always be there for me.

CHAPTER 17

Kibbutz

Even though we started to feel like family at home, we never took any vacations together. Mom hated traveling, maybe because it brought back memories of the death marches she had suffered in during the last part of the war. However, our trip to Kibbutz Ein Shemer near the southern Carmel Mountains was an exception. Mom decided to join Dad and me on this trip to see their friends, Ignatz and Ida Cohen. In fact, this was the only time she came along. This togetherness was one of the happiest times of my childhood.

My parents had known Ignatz and Ida from Poland. The Cohens had moved to Israel before World War II. They had a daughter named Orit, who was exactly my age – fourteen. Orit and her parents would occasionally come to Tel Aviv and visit us. Orit and I hit it off right from the start. She had invited me many times to come to the kibbutz, but my parents always had an excuse to turn down the invitation. At last my parents agreed to go to Ein Shemer for a couple of days. Orit and her parents were waiting for us at the gate when we got off the bus from Tel Aviv. She couldn't wait to show me around.

"Where do you want to go first?" she asked me. I wanted to see everything. We started with the communal dining room, a large hall big enough to accommodate more than 200 people.

The main attraction in the dining room (other than the food) was the bulletin board, which detailed all the rotating job duties for the residents of the kibbutz. At the time, all the cooking and dining was done in the dining room, which freed women from cooking for their family and enabled them to work wherever needed on the kibbutz.

Orit then took me to see the fields and orchards. Then she showed me the cows, chickens, horses and other livestock. I was not delighted by the smells and asked to see her room. I was strictly a city girl.

At this point, Orit took me to see her living quarters. At that time, kibbutz children lived in children's quarters and not with their parents. Things have changed since then. As we entered the room, I noticed four beds. I was puzzled. "Orit," I asked, "don't you have your own room?"

She said very matter-of-factly, "No, of course not. We all share rooms. We sleep four in a room – two boys and two girls."

I was shocked. Boys and girls sleeping in one room! "Where am I going to sleep?" I asked nervously.

"You'll sleep in Sara's bed. She went to her grandma for the weekend."

"What about the boys? Where will they sleep while I am here?

Trying to reassure me, Orit replied, "The boys will sleep in the same room with us." However, her statement had the opposite effect.

"How will I dress and undress when the boys are in the room?"

"That's easy, you ask them to turn to the wall," she replied logically.

I couldn't believe her reply, but I was too embarrassed to object. I didn't want to be the oddball again.

The next day, when we were getting ready to take a shower, I noticed boys in the girls' area. I asked Orit, "What are the boys doing here?"

Orit said; "Boys and girls take showers together here. We are all like brothers and sisters."

"Are you serious? You don't expect me to take a shower with you and the boys!"

She was taken aback by my strong reaction. She didn't understand where I was coming from. To her, it seemed very natural. After all, she had been born on the kibbutz and spent her entire life there. "Wait until we are done and then you can have the place to yourself," said Orit.

And that's what I did. I waited until they had finished taking their showers. Only then, after checking that nobody was peeking, did I dare to undress and shower.

I realized that I longed for some privacy. All this togetherness, being surrounded non-stop by people was a novelty that I had enjoyed at first, but it soon became overwhelming.

Orit and her friends included me in all their activities. We woke up well before dawn, as early as 4 am. We dressed silently, so as not to wake the children still sleeping in the adjoining rooms. We put on work boots, shorts, T-shirts and hat and waited for an adult to give us a ride to the orchards in a pick up truck. There we climbed ladders and helped pick apples, placing them into pails. When the pails were full, another adult would take them and empty the contents into a crate. It was a new experience for me, a city girl. I couldn't wait to tell my friends about my exciting summer adventures.

At 8 am, we returned to the kibbutz on a tractor. Our job for that day was done. It was getting too hot to work. It was already 27° Celsius that early in the morning. The tractor let us off in front of the kibbutz dining room, where we were about to eat breakfast and which was bustling with action. Some people were coming from work and some were just starting the day. The bulletin board displaying the work schedule for the day was crowded. On the long tables were big baskets of tomatoes and cucumbers with oil, vinegar, salt and pepper – all the necessary ingredients for an Israeli salad.

Everything else you had to get for yourself. It was self-service. There was not much of a selection, but when you are hungry, you are not very fussy. Swimming in the pool was our next stop, where the fun part of our summer day began. The main meal was served at 2 pm, and at around 3 pm, we went back to our room to rest; 3–5 pm was siesta time. The heat was so intense that it seemed that the whole world came to a standstill.

At five o'clock we would go to Orit's parents' home for cake and fruit, and stay there until the evening. My parents had spent their day with the Cohens, having a good time as well. It was great to see Mom and Dad relaxing and enjoying themselves.

Late at night we children would make a campfire, eat roasted potatoes, sit on the grass and sing songs. It was a wonderful summer. I believed Orit and her friends really liked me; they included me in everything they did. I felt a real sense of belonging.

Once I got back to Tel Aviv, I started to feel sick. I had terrible back pains. I had to run to the bathroom all the time. My mother took me to the clinic to see a specialist. After some inquires, he determined that I had a bladder infection. My bladder problems could be traced back to the time I had lain naked in the cold cellar as an infant.

Cold weather always has that effect on me, pain in my lower back – a souvenir from the war. Just when I thought I was like everyone else, the pain reminded me that I was not.

CHAPTER 18

High School Graduation

My high school graduation was simple and unpretentious, reflecting the pioneer lifestyle in Israel at the time. It was not as extravagant an affair as high school graduations today, and certainly not like the ones in the US today. There were no pomp and ceremony, no caps and gowns, speeches, or prom. I first saw that after I settled in the US. There was no graduation ceremony; the diplomas were sent through the mail. Instead of a prom, we had a party at the home of one of the graduating students.

However, my graduation was a personal milestone. It was not so much about my academic achievements, but more about the feeling that I finally belonged. I was distancing myself from Inka, the Polish refugee, and becoming Ina, the young Israeli woman. It was a slow but steady transformation.

My parents promised to buy me a dress in a fine store, and I counted down the days. On graduation day, I wanted not only to feel proud, but also to look beautiful.

The day to buy the dress finally arrived. My father and I agreed to go shopping in the late afternoon, so that my mother could join us after work. We went to the finest ladies' apparel store in Tel Aviv – Genia's, in the Allenby Street shopping district, right smack in the center of town. Dad and I stood outside for an hour waiting for Mom. Closing time was approaching. There was no sign of her!

I was in tears. "She probably forgot we were waiting for her! You know how she forgets to wake up in the morning!" I said bitterly.

My father tried to comfort me. "You know your mother would not forget your graduation. She probably was held up by an emergency," he argued.

"Come on, Dad! You know her patients always come before me!" I complained passionately.

"You don't really believe that nonsense! Don't you know how much your mother loves you? I'm sure there is a good explanation for this. Let's go into the store and see if you can find a dress you like."

We went into Genia's without Mom and bought the dress of my dreams. It was an exquisite delicate organza fabric with a design of lovely green leaves and small yellow flowers. Green was my favorite color at that time. It had a sheer petticoat underneath.

My mother finally arrived, just as we were about to leave. She tried to explain that she had been tied up with a patient, but it was too late as far as I was concerned. I didn't want to hear her explanations. I didn't care anymore.

Walking home, I looked Mom straight in the eyes and exploded, "I wish I was your patient rather than your daughter!" Sensing my mood, Mom remained silent.

Everyone loved my dress at the graduation party and said that I looked very pretty.

CHAPTER 19

Army Years

Even though I overcame many obstacles, I was still sheltered and immature. I was sick of school and books. I longed for a change. The army seemed to offer an exciting challenge. At the time, a two-year service in the IDF (Israel Defense Forces) was mandatory for every eighteen-year-old boy and girl. Israeli society looked down on young people who tried to dodge military service. I saw it as the ultimate proof of becoming a *sabra*, especially having Yitzhak Rabin as a cousin. He was already a rising star in the army.

However, at home nothing changed. The Holocaust still overshadowed our lives. It held me back. I should have been excited when my parents finally put their books about the Holocaust on shelves, creating a Holocaust library. They had kept them in storage in a wooden chest for 14 years! I know my parents expected me to show interest and read the books. I refused. I rebelled. It was my way of saying, "No! I am a different generation. I am an Israeli! I will serve in the army. I am ready to fight the enemy for my country."

Their preoccupation with the Holocaust was constant – it never ceased. Stories of survival during the Holocaust continued as a major topic of every family affair. I found them hopelessly tragic and depressing. I decided to turn a deaf ear whenever a discussion about the Holocaust began. I refused to listen time and again to the horror stories that often ended in death. I wanted to live fully in the present and look forward to a bright future.

I now regret that silly and childish behavior. I had boys on my mind instead of listening to a lesson in history. How I wish I could turn the clock back and record those survival stories! Alas, many survivors are dead now, and they took their stories with them to the grave.

Meanwhile, I was getting ready for my military service. It filled me with immense pride. I could not wait to shed my civilian clothes and get into uniform.

My first day at military camp was different from anything I had ever experienced. This camp was strictly for girls. We were girls from all walks of life, away from home for the first time. I had mixed feelings. I was a little scared, and yet excited for what was yet to come.

I looked around me – there were a few familiar faces. I saw two or three girls I knew from Tel Aviv who had graduated from high school the same year I did. That was comforting. We were in civilian clothes about to receive our uniforms. I tried mine on. The blouse was too big. I exchanged it for a smaller size. I wasn't going to have another ugly uniform like the one in high school. This time the green uniform complemented my shapely figure. I couldn't wait for my parents and friends to see the new me.

The six weeks of basic training turned out to be an unforgettable experience. After receiving our uniforms, I went to the barrack that was to be my home for the next few weeks. It was a big, long barrack with two rows of beds. My bed was right in the middle on the left side as you entered the huge barrack. The sergeant showed us how make the beds correctly, which was not very difficult since I was accustomed to making my bed at home before going to school. Even at the Roztropowiczes, I used to make my bed at the age of five. I was not really spoiled, even by Israeli standards. The sergeant told us the rules, as well as the consequences if we did not follow them. She dictated our every move. Home seemed very far away.

We were woken at 4 am. Within three minutes, we had to be outside, ready for roll call. A loud announcement on the camp's intercom would signal the beginning of a busy day. The sergeant would come in, turn all the lights on and wake us up by yelling and rushing us to dress and get ready for the morning's activity. We worked in groups. We learned how to assemble a gun in moments and how to clean and maintain it. We crawled under a barbed wire obstacle while holding a gun above the ground. I worked in the kitchen, serving the meals and cleaning pots so big I had to climb inside them in order to scrub them properly. We practiced crossing a river with the aid of a rope. Most of the difficult physical training was done early in the morning, before it became intolerably hot. It was smoldering desert weather; the temperature often reached 43°C. Nothing moved. Every living thing searched for shelter in the shade. We too, found a place in the shade, studying academic military subjects.

At 7 pm, supper was served. On arrival at the camp, I received a metal container – a mess kit. I had no idea what it was for, but we were required to bring it to the dining room for all meals. I stood in line, and when my turn came the cooks would dump the food into the mess kit. Army food resembled hospital food – it had no flavor and did not look very appealing. I ate it in order to survive and learned to appreciate homemade food. I swore I would never again make a face at the food that my mother served me at home.

Mail was a big event. Girls would line up by the mailman to see if they got letters. One day, my girlfriend Shifra came running to my tent yelling that I had a package from home. My parents had sent me a letter, as well as the kind of treats that you could not get at the base canteen. Mom had wrapped every item she sent in a napkin on which she had written, "I love you." It made me homesick.

Free time was precious. It was the chance to get to know each other. We talked about our family, friends, fashion, make up and, most importantly, boys. We would gather in a small tent. One evening, a girl brought a packet of cigarettes. She passed one burning cigarette for each of us to inhale and get the taste. I tried it. I inhaled and got a headache, and I decided right there that cigarettes were not for me.

The heat, combined with dirt and humidity, did not do much for my complexion or for my hair, which became greasy and frizzy. Unlike my dress uniform, the training clothes – baggy khaki pants and a thick cotton shirt – were not flattering to my figure. My romantic fantasy about the army soon was shattered. I hated the way I looked and felt and was ready to accept my parents for who they were and even came to appreciate them.

Water is a scarce commodity in Israel. Showering was one of the few pleasures we had. It was cool and refreshing. We would sit on the bed, feeling nice and clean, and enjoy a private moment. We'd absorb the day's events and write notes to our loved ones.

Our six weeks of basic training came to an end. Each person was assigned to a different unit. I was assigned to an office job in the Jaffa branch of Haga, the Civilian Defense Corps, which was about a half an hour from home. I could live at home and commute every day to my unit. Once a month I had to stay on the base for the weekend to guard. I served there for two years. It was a valuable learning experience. The army totally changed me from an immature teenager into a responsible adult.

I remember in particular one weekend that I had to stay on the base. I was disappointed because I had great plans for that weekend. The long afternoon hours dragged by on Saturday when suddenly I could hear my friend Simona calling my name, "Ina! Ina! There is a lady downstairs looking for you."

I ran to the street to see who it was. It was my mother! "Mom, what are you doing here?" I asked.

She said, "I know you were invited to a party, but because you couldn't come home, I brought the party to you. I bought lots of drinks and food and brought it here in a taxi (my parents never owned a car), so you can celebrate with your friends on base!"

I could not believe that she had done this for me. I felt tears well up in my eyes. I hugged and kissed her and thanked her for this unexpected wonderful surprise. I called everyone on base (about six people) to come down and help me carry all the wonderful refreshments upstairs.

My friends were moved by her gesture; they had never experienced such a kind and generous act. They did not know how to thank my mother. I felt so special to have such a thoughtful and wonderful parent. We danced to music and then sat down around the table to enjoy the delicious food. It turned out to be a great Saturday night after all!

During my army service, a major moral and political debate was raging in Israel: should Israel as a state agree to take reparations payments from Germany for the Holocaust victims? Furthermore, should Holocaust survivors take restitution for their murdered family victims?

These questions were raised by the then Prime Minister of Israel, David Ben Gurion. Chancellor Konrad Adenauer of Germany was eager to pay the restitutions, in order for Germany to gain back a respectful place among the civilized nations. Ben Gurion's strongest argument for taking the money was that Israel needed it to absorb the hundreds of thousands of Jews pouring into the new country.

There were strong arguments for and against. In my family, Mom was adamantly opposed to taking any restitution money from the Germans. She said, "I refuse to take blood money for my dead parents and brother!" She never deviated from her position on this painful issue.

My father was more pragmatic, arguing that they should take the restitution money. "Whether you take the money or not, it will not bring back the dead."

My mother could not be moved in this regard. Lawyers and other people in the community would come to our home to try to convince her. They mentioned the thousands of dollars she would be entitled to in order to try to change her mind. They all failed. She would not hear of it.[10]

I wanted desperately to be just a normal teenager, not having to deal with such difficult problems.

Adolf Eichmann's trial brought the Holocaust to the Israeli headlines once more. It became the main topic in every household in Israel. Eichmann played an important role in organizing the "Final Solution to the Jewish Question" – he was in charge of organizing the deportations of Jews from much of Europe. After the war he escaped from Germany and went to live in hiding in Argentina. In 1960, he was captured by the Mossad, the Israeli secret services. We soldiers all followed the trial breathlessly. We heard the horror stories of survivors again and again. The trial ended in a conviction and death sentence, which was upheld in the appeal to the Supreme Court. Following Eichmann's execution in 1962, his body was cremated and his ashes spread over the Mediterranean Sea, beyond Israel's territorial waters. Israel is a country that has no capital punishment with the exception of Nazi war criminals.

Along with other young men and women of my generation, I was forced to struggle with the subject of the Holocaust. It was so horrific and devastating that I chose to make it a sad part of Jewish history but that had nothing to do with me. I pretended it did not affect me personally, living in Israel.

10 Eventually, in the 1970s when I was already living in the United States, my father alone received German restitution payments. My mother stuck to her guns and never filed for it. [SH]

CHAPTER 20

College Days

Two years in the army also changed my outlook on education. I was determined to go to college. I remember how I enrolled at the Hebrew University of Jerusalem. This made me extremely proud; it was the best university in Israel and I was accepted thanks to my high matriculation scores.

The campus was situated across from the Knesset (the Israeli Parliament). It was a brand new, very modern campus, with large green lawns, trees and flowers. It was the most beautiful place I had ever seen.

It was also a very busy place. Young students rushed to classes from one building to another. Some read on the grass while others held passionate discussions. I was excited to be part of it. It was the first time I had mingled with students from all over the world, including Africa and the United Sates.

Until that point in my life, I had never realized how important it was to know other languages. Traveling to other countries was not like it is now – it was expensive and very limited. There were high taxes on travel, and restrictions on the amount of money you could take out of the country. Enemies surrounded us – we were isolated. At university, I met young people from all over the world. I discovered that the Holocaust did not take center stage for others the way it did in my home.

Even though my parents struggled financially, I was never deprived. They paid for my private high school and college, never allowing me to work. Only now do I understand the sacrifices they made for me.

118 LOCKED IN THE DARKNESS

The concept of a young working girl was alien in those days. A family friend suggested to my father that he arrange a summer job for me at the Hamashbir department store in Tel Aviv. I was taken aback by my father's strong reaction.

"My daughter working at Hamashbir? No way! Are you implying I can't provide her with all her needs?" He was clearly offended.

By the same token, it never occurred to my parents to pay me an allowance for the chores I did around the house. I never knew you could be compensated for work at home. I learned what an allowance was only when I came to the US. How I wish I had known about it then.

I was hoping to live in the dormitories, since it was cheaper than renting a room in a private home. As Jerusalem was an hour from Tel Aviv, I certainly was not going to commute every day, especially since I didn't have a car. However, foreign students were given priority for the dormitories, so I had to rent a room from a family. To cover the costs, I found a roommate named Batia, who was in her second year at college when we met.

I chose English Literature and Political Science as my majors, but it was a struggle. I remember the first lecture in English literature. It was impossible to take notes and keep up. Growing up in Israel, I knew that learning English was very important. For my classes in Medieval English Literature I needed to learn basic terms in Christianity. Even though I had lived in a Catholic household when I was a young child, I did not remember anything. Terms like "the Trinity," "the Seven Deadly Sins" and "the Virgin Mother" were alien to me.

Political Science was not any easier. All the bibliographies were in English. I spent many hours sitting in the library with a dictionary translating everything I read into Hebrew. I became a very good speller thanks to that. With time, I gained a solid understanding of the English language. Little did I know then how instrumental it would be for me later, when I met my future husband.

I had grown up without television and, for a long time, without a telephone. That was another reason for my parents having such a huge influence on me. Nevertheless, I read very much. Books were not only entertainment; they were my windows to the world.

Were my college years a great learning experience? No doubt. Was it the happiest time of my life? I am not sure. On the outside, I was like everyone else. I tried to fit in and it seemed like I did. Only deep inside, I knew I really didn't. After my relationship with my first boyfriend Zeevik ended, I did not date much. I was shy. I found it difficult to feel comfortable with the outgoing and very confident Israelis.

One day when I was sitting in the library studying for a test, a tall handsome man sat down next to me. I recognized him from my political science class. He introduced himself and proceeded to ask me some questions regarding the upcoming test. We soon started to talk about other subjects. He must have enjoyed our conversation, because at lunchtime he said "Why don't you come over to my place tonight? I'll make supper, and then we can study for the exam together."

He seemed nice and genuine. I liked the attention, and I was flattered by his invitation. I accepted. With my notes in hand, serious and ready to study, I arrived promptly. We ate a light supper, and then we sat on the couch. As soon as we had settled down he began kissing me. Before I knew what was happening, he proceeded to unbutton my blouse. It took quite a struggle to free myself from his powerful embrace. Obviously he had a different agenda for that evening than I did. In tears I said I wanted to go home. He was angry and unapologetic. The nicest thing he did was send me home in a cab.

I was upset by the experience. He really had no interest in getting to know me. I discovered I was still was on shaky ground emotionally. I was hurt. I realized I was still very vulnerable, and not as self confident as I thought I was.

After that incident, I rarely stayed in Jerusalem to socialize on weekends. Every Friday I went to Tel Aviv where I felt safe, and commuted back on Monday. It brought back the unsettling feeling that I still did not really belong, no matter how hard I tried.

It was in my last year in college that I met Avram at a party. Avram had just finished law school. I noticed him as soon as I entered the room. He was talking to a friend, and our eyes met. He was tall and handsome, with brown hair, brown eyes and a beautiful smile. Before I had a chance to sit down, he asked me to dance. We danced and talked all night. We felt mutual attraction. He was my first serious boyfriend. We dated for over a year, beginning during my last year of college and continuing after graduation.

One night when we were talking about our lives, I explained to Avram how my parents and I were reunited after being separated during the war. He made a remark that shook me.

"How do you know they are really your parents?"

I had never really thought about it. I had always accepted what my parents had told me. I never questioned their story. I was speechless. I was stunned by the idea Avram had just brought up and stood there for a while in silence.

I thought, "I don't really know. What proof do I have that they are my parents? It is so fundamental to trust your parents." It never occurred to me to doubt them. Loudly, I told Avram in a nonchalant way, "Of course they are my parents! Whatever made you think they aren't? What a ridiculous idea!"

I dismissed the incident, and never gave it another thought. I was busy living my life. I was enjoying myself. The past was the past. I wasn't going to let anything from the past get in the way of my present life.

We talked, went to the movies, danced and went on trips with friends. I remember our trip with three other couples to Lake Kinneret in the Galilee. We built our own tent right by the lake. At night we swam in the water. We cooked potatoes over a bonfire, sang songs and held heated discussions on various subjects. It was all so romantic and innocent. All eight of us slept together in the same tent and told jokes until late at night. We were young, and had great dreams for our future.

CHAPTER 21

Back to Europe

The first year in college was a struggle, but I managed to pass all my finals. My reward was a trip to Europe. This was going to be my first venture outside of Israel. I was going to visit Great Britain, France and Italy. I would not be traveling alone – my friend Edna was coming with me.

When we were discussing the trip, my mother mentioned her sister Hala and said, "This is a good chance for you to meet my family in Poland."

Poland was behind the Iron Curtain, part of the Communist Bloc during the Cold War. Before the war it had a population of 3,500,000 Jews. After the Holocaust, only 250,000 had survived. Most of them emigrated to Israel or to the US. My Aunt Hala's family was among the 20,000 Jews remaining in Poland. Her husband truly believed that the fate of the Jews in Poland would improve under the Communist regime.

My mother could not correspond with her sister in Warsaw, because receiving letters from Israel would have put Hala's family at risk. All mail from Israel was censored. The recipients could be accused of being Zionist spies, even though the two countries had diplomatic relations.

I agreed it was a good opportunity to see the family in Poland. We decided I would go to Poland if I could get a visa.

I applied for a visa at the Polish consulate in Tel Aviv. As the time of my departure approached, there was still no word regarding my request. Finally, I called the consulate to try to find out what happened to my request. I was told it took time. They advised me to pick up the visa at the Polish Embassy in London when I got there.

I remember how my father's eyes filled with tears when we said good-bye before I boarded the plane to Europe. He was so sentimental; I was going to miss him.

My trip to Italy and France was an exciting and unforgettable experience. Edna and I had a great time in London. I almost hated to take the time to go to the Polish consulate for the visa. At the consulate, the clerk said, "You need to pay $75 for your stay in a hotel in Warsaw."

"But I will be staying with my family in Warsaw. That is the purpose of my trip!" I protested.

The clerk was not moved by my objection, and continued calmly, "You still need to pay for a hotel." I was furious. It was a lot of money for a poor Israeli student, but I knew how important this visit was for Mom. So I paid, and got the visa. I said good-bye to my friend Edna, and boarded the plane to Poland.

Arriving in Warsaw was very depressing after touring Western Europe. It was dark and gloomy compared to the cheerful and busy airports I had seen before. The streets were empty. There were hardly any cars. There were no department stores with glittering lights or sidewalk cafés bustling with life. I had to remind myself that I had come here to see my family, so it did not matter. My Uncle Władek and Aunt Hala Daszkiewicz were warm and made me feel right at home with them and with their son Rysio. I speak Polish and therefore was able to communicate with them.

It was September, season of the Jewish High Holidays. Even though in Israel I had had some issues attending Orthodox religious services, here I suddenly felt the need to be with fellow Jews in the synagogue. Hala's family did not observe the Jewish holidays, mainly because the communists frowned upon religious worship. Uncle Władek had an important position in the government, in the Ministry of Labor I believe. Rysio was designated to walk me to the synagogue, but he refused to do it so as not to be seen near a synagogue. So I did not attend synagogue services on the High Holidays. I felt terrible that even after the Holocaust they still had to hide their Jewishness.

The situation of the Jews in Poland made me determined to go visit Auschwitz. I wanted to see it because I felt I owed it to my parents and, even more, to the million Jews slaughtered there. My aunt and I traveled to

Kraków, and from there we took the train to the town of Oświęcim (Auschwitz in German). Our train was traveling on the same railroad tracks as those that had taken Jews from all over Europe to their deaths. I was well acquainted with the facts of the Holocaust, but nothing could have prepared me for what I was about to see: hundreds of suitcases, shoes and eyeglasses torn from the victims' faces; lamps made of human skin. It was so overwhelmingly appalling and shocking that it made me understand the enormity of the atrocities that took place there.

Auschwitz left me upset, sick and traumatized. It moved me to the core. Some deep, deep-rooted gloom inside me responded to what I saw. It was as if I had experienced it already a long time ago. I wanted to go back home to my life in Israel. I was happy to leave Poland and what it stood for.

CHAPTER 22

Back Home

Two years later, my parents were walking hand-in-hand to attend my college graduation. It took place in the Binyanei Ha'umah Convention Center in Jerusalem, where many important events take place in Israel. I was about to receive my Bachelor's degree. I wore a beautiful two-piece white Chanel suit. Dad wore his dark blue Shabbat suit, and Mom had on her lovely black dress. It was a triumphant moment for me. I had come a long way, overcoming many obstacles since my arrival from Poland. And I had now mastered English as well as Hebrew.

After graduation, my father encouraged me to enroll in a teacher-training program. Growing up in a home with a working mother, where I had spent so much time alone, had not been a very positive experience for me. I felt that as a teacher I would have more time for my family than she had had, so I looked for a position as an English teacher.

In 1964 I got my first job at the ORT Vocational High School for Girls, and attended the credential program at the same time. I quickly discovered I really loved children and enjoyed teaching.

Spring 1967 was a time that no one who lived in Israel could ever forget. Gamal Abdel Nasser, the Egyptian leader, supported by the Soviet Union, posed a serious threat to the existence of Israel by closing the straits of Tiran and Israel's shipping routes. He delivered hate-filled speeches against Israel, inciting the masses to attack us. I remember listening and feeling frightened at the thought that he might succeed.

Tension was rising daily. The tourists were lining up to leave our troubled country before the hostilities began. Many of us who lived in Israel feared that we might be on a sinking ship. We did not know what the next day might bring. We were ordered to cover our windows, so that there could be a total blackout in case of an attack. The streets, normally bustling with activity, were completely deserted. Tel Aviv was a ghost town.

On June 6 in the middle of the night, the day after Israel's air force destroyed the Egyptian air force on the ground, we heard an air raid siren and rushed to the cellar of our building. Every apartment house in Israel had an air raid shelter that was often in the cellar (today all new houses are built with a reinforced room as a shelter for each family). It was very scary for all of us, sitting down there, not knowing what was happening. All my life I had hated dark places, so this experience was especially chilling for me. I held on tightly to my father and tried to pass the time talking. Another siren let us know it was safe to return to our apartment.

That night was typical of the period to follow. We were glued to the radio (we still had no television), desperate to hear the daily reports about the developing situation. It seemed that war was inevitable. In this state of anxiety and uncertainty I went to bed.

The next thing I knew, somebody was shaking me and calling my name. "Inka! Inka! Wake up! Wake up!"

It was my mother urging me to open my eyes. She was so excited she could barely speak. She said, "Do you know what happened while you were sleeping? Our air force destroyed the Egyptian air force in a surprise attack on their planes on the ground. It happened at dawn. They have no air force! Can you believe it? We now have complete air superiority! The sky is ours!"

What a great relief it was to know we would not be attacked from the air. The distance between Tel Aviv and Egypt is very short. I went back to sleep feeling much safer.

The next day, the headlines of all the newspapers in the world described this brilliant military victory in great detail. Yitzhak Rabin, the Chief of Staff during the Six Day War, became a household name. It was he who was responsible for this plan and gave the order to execute it. I was so proud that he was my cousin!

Still, we were worried about Rachel, who lived on the border with Lebanon. The Syrians were constantly bombarding the settlements close to

Manara. A fierce battle with the Syrians developed. The Syrians lost the battle and had to retreat and the Golan Heights fell into Israeli hands. That whole region could now breathe easier.

I will never forget how emotional it was to see Defense Minister Moshe Dayan and my cousin Yitzhak Rabin on television walking for the first time through the main gate to Jerusalem and the Western Wall.

The old city of Jerusalem, where Jews had been denied access for so long, was under our control again. For two thousand years, whenever Jews prayed they would face Jerusalem. Even secular Jews like me took pause to reflect on the importance of this moment. These landmarks had just been liberated by Israeli soldiers. Jordan was warned not to enter the war, but they ignored the plea and initiated hostilities. They lost. It was a very proud moment for Israel and Jews around the world. The Jews had proved to be great warriors, determined never to let another Holocaust happen again.

Life went on, and my friends slowly began to get married. My boyfriend of a year and a half, Avram, graduated from law school in Tel Aviv. I attended his graduation ceremony, and was very proud of him. I was secretly hoping he would propose. I was devastated when he told me that he had been accepted to a graduate program at Cambridge University and would soon be leaving for England. Avram was serious about advancing his career. So, Avram and I parted, and he went on to do his doctorate in criminal law at Cambridge University.

I was speechless. I was heartbroken for a long time, and refused to be consoled. I dated, but I couldn't find anyone who really attracted me. I started to believe I would never fall in love again.

CHAPTER 23

Alfred

My friends and family were constantly trying to find me a match. I was twenty-eight and single. In Israel, I was already considered an old maid. In 1969, a friend of my parents introduced me to an American tourist named Alfred Heller. He was visiting family in Haifa. I agreed to meet him, but I did not expect much from the date.

It was a weekday, and I had a great excuse prepared just in case Alfred turned out to be another disappointment: I needed to get up early the next day for work. The doorbell rang. I ran to the mirror one last time to check my makeup. I was wearing a sheer white blouse with a green miniskirt (the latest fashion) and a green vest. It was an outfit I had sewn myself.

When I opened the door, I had a real surprise. Standing there was a tall, handsome man, with beautiful blue eyes and straight black hair. He was wearing an elegant, well-tailored suit. I don't know how long I let him stand there. I was stunned by what I saw. I did not expect such a "hunk." With a mischievous smile, he finally asked, "Aren't you going to let me in?"

At last I recovered and asked him to come in. He looked like Frank Sinatra. I excused myself, ran into the bathroom, and took a deep breath. I wanted to change into something more elegant but coming out in a different outfit would have looked too obvious. I returned to the living room, racking my brain for something to say in English. I prayed I would not mess up.

I didn't have to worry. Alfred was easy to talk to. He was funny and charming. The conversation flowed very naturally. He told me about his family in Haifa, and back home in the US. I told him about my life in Israel, my parents and friends – the usual small talk when two people meet. I offered to show him Tel Aviv at night. We ended up going to a coffee shop in the old city of Jaffa overlooking the Mediterranean. We found out that we had much in common. We were both from Europe – he was from Germany and I from Poland – both survived by being hidden during the war. The difference was that he had hid together with his parents. We talked a lot about the war. We both were deeply affected by it. Alfred shared with me what it was like hiding in a deserted building in Brussels, and how especially difficult it had been for a young person.

This is what Alfred told me about his family.

Alfred's Story

Saul and Gisela Heller were born in Munich, Germany. Their parents had moved to Germany from Galicia, Poland (today in Ukraine) early in the twentieth century. The German Jews who lived in Germany looked down on the Eastern European Jews who arrived there later. The former were already assimilated; they went to German schools, worked for German companies and dressed like Germans. Alfred grew up as an acculturated Jew in Germany. Of course, in the end it didn't matter; all the Jews faced the same fate under Hitler.

Alfred's parents had a shoe store in Munich. After the Nazis came to power in 1933 and the persecution of the Jews began, the family decided to flee to Belgium to find refuge. They found an abandoned apartment in Brussels and decided to live there. Since they had entered Belgium illegally, Saul and Gisela had no papers identifying them as legal residents. As a result, the Hellers did not receive food stamps that entitled them to buy rations (due to food shortages). In order to survive, there was no other way but to steal food. During the war, Alfred, who was about thirteen years, became responsible for providing food for his parents.

Alfred's older brother, Ernst, was caught and deported by the Germans in 1942 or 1943. Believing Nazi assurances of work and better living conditions, he boarded a train for what he thought was going to be a labor camp. It turned out it was a train to a mass murder site. He was never heard from again.

Alfred did not "look Jewish." He had that desirable "Aryan" look – blue eyes. He would run to the stores and steal food. He was a lifesaver to his parents. They could never have survived the war without him.

One incident that Alfred recalled occurred one day when he was returning from his Jewish school, carrying his book in his hands. A German soldier stopped him and said, "How old are you?" Alfred answered, "I'm thirteen years old." The soldier said, "I have a son your age. He is in Germany with his mother." He stroked Alfred's hair and handed him a loaf of bread. Then the soldier turned to Alfred again and asked, "Can you show me the book you are studying from?"

Alfred handed the soldier his book. When the soldier realized that it was a Hebrew book, he grabbed the loaf of bread from Alfred's hands and started to curse and yell, "*Jude! Jude!*" Poor Alfred took off and started running as fast as he could, fearful for his life.

Wedding photo, Sabina and Alfred Heller with Sabina's parents,
the Goszczewskis, March 9, 1970

I could see Alfred reliving these horrible events as he related them to me.

At the time I had no idea I had just met the greatest salesman ever. Alfred knew how to talk. That was his occupation. He knew how to sell himself to me. I was buying whatever he was selling. It was love at first sight. We had the best time together. We became inseparable for the next three months.

At the end of the third month, he had to go back to the US. We kept in touch by letter and phone. Then Alfred suggested I come visit him in California. I was teaching high school, and I could not leave in the middle of the year. Another problematic issue was that Alfred insisted he wanted to continue living in the US. If I was seriously considering marrying him, I would have to leave Israel, my parents, my family and my friends. It was a difficult decision.

We know now that Alfred won that argument. Once the issue was settled, we decided to get married. The wedding took place in Tel Aviv (his concession to me) on March 9, 1970. Soon after the wedding, I quit my teaching position at ORT and moved with my husband to Los Angeles, California.

My wedding photo reflects the way my parents felt about my departure to the US. My father looks more somber than cheerful at the wedding ceremony. They were not thrilled to send me so far away, but they did not want to stand in the way of my happiness. They felt it was in my best interest to let me go. They made every effort not to show their feelings of gloom to my face.

CHAPTER 24

Life in Los Angeles

Alfred had to return to Los Angeles earlier than planned, so I stayed behind for another week. When I arrived, I had no idea what to expect. So far everything had been so romantic. I hadn't had time to give it serious thought. I had lived most of my life in Israel. I did not have the faintest idea what life in Los Angeles would be like.

Alfred picked me up at the airport. We stayed in a hotel for a few days until we could move to our own apartment in Westwood. The first morning in LA, I opened the window and looked outside. I had to hold my breath! There were *four* lanes of traffic on Wilshire Blvd. I had never seen so many cars on the street. The traffic was so congested! And this was 1970. The traffic was a fraction of what it is now.

I felt like an ant in this huge metropolis. I began to see how different LA was from Tel Aviv. There was nobody to talk to. Everyone was in a rush. Shopping was different. In Israel, we'd shopped at a small grocery store, where you met your neighbors and where the shopkeeper knew you well. Here, nobody knew me; you could shop for years in a market and the chances were you would not run into anybody you knew.

In LA, no one walks up and down the streets, unlike in Tel Aviv. Where were the sidewalk cafes full of beautiful people sipping ice cold drinks? All you saw were cars. This is still very disturbing to me, even after having lived in Los Angeles here for 42 years. I miss the hustle and bustle of the people on the sidewalks.

In Israel, life was casual and informal. You could get together with a friend in a café any day of the week for a little chitchat over a cup of coffee.

I needed to learn to drive, because no one walked in Los Angeles. It was so spread out! In Tel Aviv (then), everything was within walking distance. Life moved at a much slower pace in Israel. People had more time to visit each other.

Missing my family, I was anxious to meet my husband's. They threw a few parties in our honor. That was it. Afterwards, I found his relatives to be prim, proper and formal. You could not visit them without being invited, because an invitation meant a formal dinner. That involved much work, so invitations were rare.

Sometimes it seemed like I had come from a different planet. My family in Israel lived there for many years without a phone. In 1951, when we moved to our own apartment, there were no telephone lines in the area at all. Life did not stop because of that. People would drop in without calling. If company showed up unexpected, you would straighten up the living room and invite them in. Life was not complicated. Here in the United States everyone guarded their privacy so fiercely that they lost touch with people.

I was the new kid on the block one more time. It was a role I knew how to play. I had to do it all over again and work very hard to fit in with the new way of life. Adjusting to new situations was something I had been doing all my life.

A week after my arrival from Israel, Alfred informed me that he had to go back to work. I was disappointed. I was awakened to reality and soon realized that I was lost in LA without a car in LA.

I spent much of my first year in LA crying. After years of struggling in Israel to adjust and fit in and feel like I belonged, I had to find my way in a new country all over again. It was something I had to do on my own. I had become dependent on my husband to take me everywhere; now I started to take the bus, and for the first time experienced LA's inefficient public transportation. It felt more like a nightmare than a dream.

I learned to drive and got my license. That was liberating. It was the first step in taking control of my life again.

At home, I had to prove I could make a meal for my husband. I learned how to cook. My mother was not much of a role model. She was a professional, not much of a homemaker. I bought cookbooks and began to experiment with different recipes. My kitchen started to look like a laboratory. I was busy, but not busy enough. I still had to face a long day alone until my husband came home from work.

In desperation, I decided to look for a job. But what could I do? Even though my English was good, it was not good enough. I was also very self-conscious of my accent. I thought that perhaps I could teach Hebrew, and after making several calls I got a part-time job teaching Hebrew in the Stephen S. Wise Reform Temple. I made friends there and things began to look up.

I met some of Alfred's friends. They were Holocaust survivors who had arrived in the US after World War II. We were all making our new homes in America, the land of opportunities. It has been said that America was no longer a melting pot, but a salad bowl – you could be an American without giving up your culture. This is what we found with our friends.

We started our family. In 1971, Ron was born. I became busy learning to be a mother. Then, five years later, Mark was born. My life revolved around my sons and my husband. I decided to stay home with my kids, knowing from my own sad memories of being left alone so much how important that was. I was content having my family around me. I felt more detached than ever from the Holocaust.

I stayed home for ten years. When Mark turned three years old, I got a part time job teaching Hebrew in Temple Judea, which was only five minutes from our home. We also joined the synagogue as well as a *Havura*, a Jewish social group of young married couples with children. I also made new friends with some of my colleagues who taught with me, most of whom were also Israeli.

My parents, who lived in Israel, were getting old. My mother had a stroke and a few years later my father developed Parkinson's Disease. When they came to visit I was shocked to see my father's deteriorated condition. His hands were shaking and his speech was slurred. After crying for days, I took him to see a neurologist who gave him medication to control the disease. My father took the medication for two months, and all his symptoms disappeared. We were thrilled with the results, and my father returned to Israel feeling well again.

In 1986 my father died of heart disease. After his death I brought my mother to Los Angeles to stay with me. She lived in Los Angeles for another eleven years, and when she passed away in 1997, I took her body to Israel and had her buried in Holon, next to my father as she had requested.

In 1987 I contracted cancer of the bile duct and survived, which is quite rare. Maybe I was meant to live and find my past.

CHAPTER 25

Reunion

About a month after my discovery of the missing part of my life, I felt the need to call the Roztropowiczes and perhaps even meet them one day. They could provide more details than I had read in the documents. I was so curious. I wanted to know everything about them – their family and especially their parents. I found out that the three Roztropowicz sisters now lived in Warsaw and the brother on a ranch in the south of Poland, close to the Czech border.

With the encouragement of my family and friends, I decided to call Poland. It did not happen overnight. I kept talking about it. I hesitated, scared of having to converse in Polish, but that was only an excuse. In reality I was terrified of what else I might discover.

I was extremely nervous. My hands were shaking when I dialed their number in January 2000. In a way I was hoping they would not answer the phone. The phone rang three times, and then a woman's voice answered: "Roztropowicz residence."

I held my breath. After what seemed like eternity I blurted, "This is Inka from Los Angeles."

Stanka exclaimed, "We have been waiting for your call for sixty years!" Then she called loudly to her sister, "It's Inka!" Then she sighed and said, "I wish my mother were here to talk to you. She got sick after she had dropped you off in the orphanage. She never recovered from that separation. She talked about you till the day she died." Natalia passed away on June 20, 1954

Amazingly, my Polish came back and I was able to talk – hesitantly at first, but I gained more confidence with each sentence.

Stanka wanted to know everything about me. "What do you look like now? Are you married? Tell me about your husband. Do you have children? Tell me about your children. Where do you live? What do you do?"

Of course, I wanted to know everything about their lives, too. We decided to correspond and exchange pictures to see what we looked like almost sixty years since we had last seen each other.

There was so much information on which to catch up; I could not absorb it all. It was not important. What mattered was that I could feel the warmth and affection for me in her voice. I knew deep in my heart that this was the beginning of something very wonderful and important for me. It could not have happened at a better time in my life. I was still grieving over the loss of my mother and husband.

I was ecstatic. I told everyone my incredible life story. We were corresponding. We were talking on the phone. We were getting to know each other. I was not alone in the world. I had gained a new family.

CHAPTER 26

Reunited at Last

I was looking for a way to show my gratitude to my newly re-found family. I called Yad Vashem in Jerusalem and asked to talk to the department for the Righteous Among the Nations – non-Jewish people who saved Jews during the war. I asked the lady who answered the phone what the procedure is to recognize a person as a Righteous Among the Nations. She said: "You need to write the story of your rescue to Yad Vashem. A committee will check it out. We have people all over the world who work for us to verify the stories and help the public committee decide whether the person deserves this highest of honors bestowed by Israel on behalf of the Jewish people."

I fulfilled the requirements. It was a lengthy process. Following the submission of the survivors' affidavits and the check for corroborative evidence, the committee meets to vote on whether to recognize the prospective candidate as one of the Righteous. Once they approve, the award is presented in a dignified ceremony at Yad Vashem, or at the Israeli embassy in the honoree's country. The family of the honoree usually attends. By now, many of the honorees are honored posthumously, since most have already passed away.

In May 2000, my phone rang. It was a long-distance call from Yad Vashem. A lady's voice asked, "May I speak to Sabina Heller?"

I answered, "This is Sabina."

"We are pleased to inform you that the Committee for the Designation

of the Righteous has approved the presentation of the award to Józef and
Natalia Roztropowicz."[11]

I was delighted! I was so pleased that the right decision had been
reached. I knew they would approve. Still, I was thrilled it actually happened.
It took sixty years, but finally I had discovered my story and *justice had been
done!* At last the Roztropowicz name would be displayed on the wall in Yad
Vashem's Garden of the Righteous. Yad Vashem is the place where every dig-
nitary or head of state that goes to Israel visits. It is where the Pope John
Paul II chose to ask the forgiveness of the Jewish people for the failings of
Catholics.

I could not wait to share the good news with the Roztropowicz family.
The ceremony would take place at the Israeli embassy in Warsaw on July 18,
2000. We started planning my visit. Of course I would attend the ceremony,
but the real reason was to reunite with my wartime family. We had a past that
we shared, but in the present we were strangers. I had so many mixed feelings;
I proceeded carefully.

During one of our phone conversations, I said to Stanka, "I would like
to stay in a hotel, somewhere close to where you live. Can you make the
reservations?"

Stanka answered, "That's not necessary. You can stay with us."

I insisted on staying in a hotel. Stanka rejected my idea. We dropped
the subject for a while. I did not feel comfortable staying with them because
I was unsure about their living conditions. I had read about families forced to
share apartments. I had heard that there was a shortage in living quarters in the
Eastern European countries. The idea of having to speak Polish all day frightened me as well. Above all, I did not really know them. We had a common
past, but that was a long time ago. We had lived in diverse worlds for so many
years and now probably had many differences. I thought it would be safer to
get to know each other from a little distance.

As the date of the trip approached, I needed to resolve the problem of
my accommodation. Stanka, being as stubborn as she was, did not want to

11 Józef and Natalia Roztropowicz were recognized on May 28, 2000; Zofia Stramska
    was honored on December 18, 2001; and the Roztropowiczes' daughters, Janina
    and Stanisława, were honored on October 23, 2002. See Yad Vashem Archives,
    M.31/8980.

hear a word about any hotel. "You are staying with us and that is final!" she exclaimed. I could tell there was no point in discussing it with her any further. Eventually, they decided I would not stay with Stanka, but with Jana, who had a larger home. Moreover, Stanka did not like to cook, but Janka was a fairly skilled cook.

I did not wish to arrive empty-handed. I wanted to bring some gifts for them, but I quickly realized that I did not really know what to buy because I did not know them at all. So we agreed that I would take them shopping when I arrived.

As the day of my trip approached, I began to feel more and more apprehensive. I was embarking on one of the most important trips of my life, the trip that would unlock my past. I was nervous, anxious, and upset with myself for agreeing to stay with my hosts. What if we did not hit it off? What if they were not waiting for me at the airport? What if I did not recognize them? What if they had gotten confused with the date? These were some of the thoughts that raced through my mind.

After tearful goodbyes from my sons Mark and Ron, I was on my way. I took a direct flight from Los Angeles to Frankfurt, Germany. During the entire sixteen-hour flight I did not talk to anyone. I could not fall asleep. I was a nervous wreck.

In Frankfurt, I transferred to the Polish airline, Lot, for the two-hour flight to Warsaw. Everyone on board spoke Polish. Flying on a Polish plane was like already being in Poland. I found myself sitting next to a lovely young Polish woman named Teresa. She turned to me and said in English, "It's so good to go home after a vacation." I wondered what to say. I was too edgy to invent a story. So I responded, "I am returning to Warsaw after sixty years to meet the Polish rescuers who saved my life during the Holocaust."

Teresa was intrigued, so I continued my story. I was happy to pass the time talking. It took my mind off worrying about the encounter with the Roztropowiczes.

"Will you stay with me in the airport until I find the Roztropowicz sisters? I hope I'll recognize them. What if they fail to show up?"

Teresa reassured me that she would stay by my side until I located them. Over the loudspeaker I heard the pilot say, "We are beginning our descent to Warsaw Airport." I excused myself and went to the restroom to change my clothes.

I had promised Stanka I would be wearing a black suit with a white T-shirt. I washed my face, trying to freshen up after the long flight. I put on some make up to look my best for the reunion and returned to my seat.

I could hear the pounding of my heart. My body was breaking out in a cold sweat. My mouth was dry as the plane came to a halt. I did not feel steady on my feet. Teresa followed me as she had promised.

The airport in Warsaw is small in comparison to Western European airports. It was not crowded; in fact, it was rather quiet. Teresa helped me with my luggage. We started to walk toward the exit. There were many relatives and friends waiting for the arriving passengers.

Three women and a man were standing in the very first row. They must have been in their seventies. They were smiling at me. One of them, the tall one with short, gray, wavy hair, glasses and a lovely big smile had a bouquet of red roses in her hands. She stepped forward and called "Inka!" We hugged and kissed, with tears in our eyes. We were unable to utter a word. I knew it was Stanka. I embraced Jana and her husband Zdzisław, as Teresa bade goodbye.

I was pleasantly surprised to discover that Jana and Zdzisław owned a car. They put my suitcase in the back of their little Fiat, and we were on our way to their apartment. I immediately noticed the many changes that had taken place since my last visit, due no doubt to the collapse of the Soviet Union.

The streets of Warsaw were now dynamic and lively. The colorful neon lights of European and American companies sparkled everywhere. It was a busy, cheerful place. People were sitting in the sidewalk cafes, enjoying good food and drinks. The windows displayed the latest fashions. The stores were well stocked with a variety of foods. None of the shortages of the past was apparent.

Jana lived on the outskirts of Warsaw, in an area called Ursus, which was quite different from Warsaw. It was a reminder of the Communist era. Here you still could see massive, gray, uniform buildings built to accommodate as many people as possible. You could not tell one building from another. The hallway walls were covered with graffiti. It was dark, as nobody had changed the burned-out light bulb. We felt our way in the darkness to Jana's apartment. Zosia, the eldest sister, opened the door for us. We kissed and hugged and cried again.

It was a small, warm and homey place. Jana showed me to the room in which I would be staying. My bed was made. Zosia rushed to the kitchen to make tea and bring some snacks and cake. We sat around the table, the five of us who used to be family. Now we were trying to catch up on the years after destiny had separated us. I was eager to hear every detail they could remember about the years I was with them. I kept staring at them to see if it brought back any memories. Unfortunately I could not recall any of the events they described. I kept staring at each one of them.

Stanka was the most outspoken. Her complexion was unusually smooth and healthy for a lady her age. She was also the most energetic and resourceful of the siblings. Her family held her in great regard. She had been a professor of agriculture, and she had even traveled to Idaho to research the potato, her specialty. In fact, she was the only one of the Roztropowiczes who had traveled outside of Poland. With her knowledge of English, she would frequently rescue me when I was at a loss for a Polish word.

I looked at her clothes. I noticed she was wearing black pants and a top, as were her two sisters. Things had changed since my last visit to Poland in 1962. The whole world dressed the same now. The differences between East and West were disappearing.

Jana was a little heavier than Stanka. Her hair was also gray, but longer and curlier. She was sitting next to her husband Zdzisław . She was more reserved and didn't say much. She sometimes whispered a few words to Zosia. They seemed to be close. When Jana talked, she spoke slowly and haltingly. She had a storyteller's talent. She would capture everybody's attention. Jana also had the reputation of being the best cook of the family. Family gatherings would always take place at her home.

Zosia was sickly at times. Jana and Zosia were both heavy smokers, which left them short of breath and gasping for air. But they were so heavily addicted that they could not stop. They all were concerned about Zosia's health and tried to care for her as best they could. Zosia was easygoing and always agreeable. All the grandchildren loved her. They would sit next to her and never leave her side. She would read them stories and was very skilled at inventing her own stories. They would sit glued to her, hanging on each word that came out of her mouth.

As I watched them, I had the strong sensation that they really knew me. I sensed that they still cared for me because of the bond created so long ago. It's difficult to explain. Perhaps it is like a mother who gives away a child and finds him many years later. The love is still there, despite all the years that have passed. I was listening to them talking, but I could not concentrate on what they were saying. All I could think was that I used to be a part of this family.

Now all the differences between us began to vanish, and the years that had gone by started to melt away. We wanted to recapture the intimacy that exists only among family members. They called me "our wartime sister." I felt we had something that nobody could take away from us, a past that linked us. I really did not know them well yet, but I had a sense that we would be a family again.

They bombarded me with questions about my life, and I was eager to tell them all the details. I began by relating what had happened to me after I left them, and slowly brought them up to date.

Overcome by exhaustion and emotions, we decided to turn in and call it a night. I fell asleep immediately and slept until noon the next day. I felt like a baby, safe and secure.

Stanka and Zosia lived separately in apartments in the center of Warsaw, across from the infamous Palace of Culture that the Soviets gave as a gift to the Poles during the Communist regime. It is a symbol of an era hated by every Pole.

The night that I arrived, both Stanka and Zosia slept in Jana's house. They all wanted to be with me!

Stanka greeted me with a smile when I woke up. She asked me to join them for breakfast after I dressed.

The bathroom was small but functional, and I was thankful there was hot running water day and night. The bathroom and the toilet were situated right next to the kitchen. It was strange to me and made me feel self-conscious. I realized that people sitting in the kitchen could hear everything going on in the bathroom.

"What a strange layout!" I thought to myself.

When I asked Jana about it, her face reflected the revulsion she felt for everything the Soviets did. "The Soviets built apartments that way to save on plumbing expenses. All water outlets were in the one area, whether it was convenient for the tenants or not," she explained.

After breakfast, I opened my suitcase full of toiletries, cosmetics and over-the-counter medications that I had brought as gifts. Friends of mine who had visited Poland said that there were still shortages of these items in Poland. It was awkward. I did not bring anything more personal simply because I did not know them.

While I was sleeping, the sisters had made plans for me to meet the rest of the family. There were children and grandchildren to meet, all of whom knew about me. It was very exciting to have an instant, large, extended family. This was a new experience for me; my parents had lost all their family in the Holocaust, and so did their friends.

On Tuesday morning we went to see Jendryk and his beautiful ranch. I was very anxious to see him, because we had played together as children. This trip had given me an opportunity to see the country I had heard so much about from my parents. They remembered prewar Poland fondly. I was curious to see the country of my ancestors for myself.

I discovered that Poland had many lakes, rivers and forests. The forests were where the underground partisans would hide during the war. On the way, we stopped to see a beautiful 16th-century castle that had belonged to a Polish nobleman. The guide showing us the place told us the following story:

The Soviet soldiers who liberated Poland after the war were peasants. They lacked the sophistication to appreciate art. The castle had a collection of paintings by famous Polish artists. One of the soldiers took a painting off the wall, cut it up, and used it as a rag to polish his shoes. When his superior found out, he was outraged and had the soldier court-marshaled.

But it wasn't only the Communists who destroyed Polish castles and buildings of historic importance. During the Communist regime, the local population also took part in looting and trashing castles. They would steal pieces of marble and sculpture to decorate their homes. You would find a piece of exquisite Italian marble that belonged in a fine castle in their bathrooms.

Past and present came together in Poland in a strange way. Now the castles were used as tourist attractions, hotels and restaurants. We decided to have our dinner at the castle. You could eat a hamburger and French fries there. But there was a certain odor typical of old churches and castles that even the smell of French fries could not mask.

We were all crammed tightly in that small car for about five hours. Even though I enjoyed the ride, I was quite happy to get out and stretch when we finally reached Jendryk's home in Doboszowice.

Jendryk was standing in front of his house leaning on his cane, waiting anxiously for us to arrive. He was the closest in age to me. I wondered if I would recall anything about him. Sadly, I didn't.

I walked briskly toward him and embraced him. He was medium-built, in his late sixties. He broke into a wide grin and his friendly blue eyes beamed with delight when he saw me. We hugged for a few seconds and I noticed tears pouring down his cheeks. He couldn't talk, but he nodded his head when I whispered in his ear, "Do you remember me?"

Jendryk had suffered a stroke a couple of years earlier. He had lost his ability to speak. His right side was weak. The latest rehabilitation methods for stroke patients had not yet reached Poland. He could only communicate his thoughts by writing them on paper, which made communication difficult and slow.

I was trying to figure out what gift would make him happy. "A lawn mower!" he informed me on the spot.

Despite his disabilities, Jendryk continued to work and take care of his ranch. His wife had passed away a few years previously. He insisted on mowing the huge lawn around his house. He showed me his ranch and all the things he was growing there with great pride. It had everything: flowers, fruit trees, vegetables and nuts. He loved to plant flowers and vegetables and watch them grow. Poles love to work their land. They consider land to be sacred. He informed me that all the food served for supper had been grown on the ranch.

He invited us inside his country-style house. He had built the house all by himself and was proud of it. Poland is very rich in forests, so wood is relatively inexpensive. The entire home was built from panels of wood.

We all sat in the kitchen for supper – Jendryk's daughter and her family, and his son and his family. As they were reminiscing about the past, we also discussed the big upcoming event — the ceremony honoring their parents as Righteous Among the Nations. It was to take place at a theater in Warsaw the following week. Three generations of Roztropowiczes were going to attend. Unfortunately, due to his stroke, Jendryk was unable to travel. I was so glad I was able to meet him then, because he passed away only three years later.

I was looking forward to the ceremony for another reason. Stanka and the other sisters told me that Natalia had written a letter addressed to me before her death. She wrote it with the hope that it would reach me one day. In that letter she explained how they had found and rescued me. It was a confirmation of my Jewish descent, my original name, and my birthday. She explained that she did not know my parents well, but she knew of them. Above all, she told me her reasoning for giving me away and asked for my forgiveness.

The sisters were going to give me the letter after the ceremony. You can imagine how anxious I was to read it! A great deal of this book is a result of that letter.

After the ceremony they were planning a big party at Stanka's home. Everyone was preparing all kinds of delicacies. I wanted to cook and help in the preparations but they refused to let me do anything. I was to remain the guest.

We spent much time talking about what we were going to wear. They put on a fashion show for me, showing me their best outfits. I discovered how modest their wardrobe was and I made a mental note of it. On my next trip, I planned to bring them some elegant clothes. My own choice of clothes was very limited. I decided to wear my perfect-for-traveling wrinkle-free black polyester suit.

July 18, 2000

The day of the Righteous Among the Nations ceremony arrived. It was a lovely summer day. We all woke up earlier than usual. Although Jendryk was unable to attend, his son Bogdan and Bodgan's wife Eva were among the first members of the family to arrive. Everybody was talking about the courage of Józef and Natalia.

Eva offered her opinion: "I have thought a lot about Józef and Natalia and their brave rescue of Inka and what I would have done in that situation. I must admit that if I had been in their place, I doubt I would have risked my family's life – especially my children's – to save an unknown child."

I overheard what she said. I felt a brief but piercing pain in my heart, but when I recovered, I realized that she was just being honest. Most people would probably feel that way. Many times I had wondered what I would have done had I been in their shoes.

Stanka commented on Eva's remark. "You don't understand. Our life was in danger even before taking in Inka. The Nazis and Bandera's gangs had been terrorizing us.[12] So we did not really feel that taking Inka in increased the threat on our lives in any way. We couldn't let an innocent baby die in such an inhuman way. We just felt that this was the right thing to do. You had to be there to understand why things happened the way they did."

When the rest of the family arrived, we lined up for a grand family photo. Then we took off in several cars, directly to the ceremony site.

The Ceremony

Many other rescuers were honored that day, but the Roztropowicz family clearly had the largest representation. They occupied most of the seats in that theater. They were all holding cameras, ready to capture this event for posterity.

The media crews started to arrive with their equipment. They positioned themselves right in front of the stage. Upon entering the theater, I immediately noticed a large flag of the State of Israel displayed beside the Polish flag. It made me feel extremely proud and safe. As long as there is a State of Israel, a Holocaust could never happen again. A Jewish state is life insurance for Jews all over the world.

As we sat down, dignitaries representing the Polish government began to arrive and take their seats. The Israeli ambassador to Poland and his interpreter walked up to the stage and sat down. We all rose to the music of the Polish national anthem. When the Israeli national anthem, *Hatikvah*, played, I sang forcefully and proudly, as if to let the Jews who perished know that we remembered them. Appropriately enough, the word *Hatikvah* means "hope" in Hebrew.

After some speeches in Polish and in Hebrew, each recipient was called to come up onto the stage. A dignitary told the story of the rescue, while the recipient received a medal and a Righteous Among the Nations Certificate in the name of the rescuer. The surviving son or daughter received the honor for

12 Stepan Bandera was a Ukrainian ultra-nationalist leader and head of the Organization of Ukrainian Nationalists (OUN), whose armed units murdered tens of thousands of Poles and Jews, especially in the former eastern Polish regions that are today part of Ukraine. Their units were commonly known as *Banderowcy*. [ed.]

their deceased mother or father. Most of the survivors were deceased as well. I was the only living survivor present.

It was Stanka's turn to receive the medal. She delivered a short speech, stressing the courage of her parents and the risk they took by rescuing me. She mentioned my name and emphasized the fact that I had come from Los Angeles to attend the ceremony.

The audience turned toward me, clapping enthusiastically. I blushed, unaccustomed to being in the public spotlight, and waved back. It was a very moving moment for me, one that I will never forget.

Stanka and other members of the family were all bombarded with questions by the media. We took pictures with the Israeli ambassador and his wife. After the ceremony I was interviewed by Polish TV, answering questions about my rescue in halting Polish.

All good things come to an end; so, too, this ceremony. Natalia and Józef Roztropowicz had finally been given the honor they deserved.

But the celebration continued at Stanka's house. The table in her living room was covered with a white tablecloth. In the center was a beautiful cake with the message, "Welcome Back, Inka!" Around it, there was a display of dishes filled with Polish sausages, various salads, meats, pierogi (stuffed dumplings), berries and plenty of alcohol to celebrate the occasion.

Oddly enough, I felt very much at home with them. I wonder if it was their warm welcome or the fact that I had just found peace of mind with my recent discoveries.

I discovered that a person's taste develops very early in life. Growing up in Israel, the fruits I ate were mostly oranges, bananas and apples. Later, when strawberries and cherries became available, I could not control my craving for berries. I loved them so much. I preferred berries to ice cream. I was baffled by my odd taste and wondered where I had developed it.

During my visit with my Aunt Hala in Poland in 1962, she asked me what foods I liked. I knew exactly what my favorite dish was – pierogi – a Polish dish that I certainly never ate in Israel. I stuffed myself with pierogi, knowing I would never have another chance to eat it in Israel.

Now it became clear to me where all these cravings had come from. They were the kinds of foods I had eaten when I was very little, living with the Roztropowicz family. The memory had stayed with me all those years.

Later, we watched the report of our event and my very short interview on television. Anything to do with World War II still evokes tremendous interest in Poland. The nation suffered oppression for so many years, first by the Nazis and later by the Soviets. They enjoy their present freedom, but they do not want to forget what happened in the not-so-distant past. The ceremony in which Israel honored the Righteous Among the Nations made the Poles very proud.

After the party, Stanka carefully pulled what looked like a very old document out of a drawer. Her hands were trembling. She turned to me and said: "I would like you to have the original letter my mother wrote in the hope that it would reach you one day."

I could tell how difficult it was for Stanka to part with the letter. It was a very moving moment. The page was yellowed, proof to the many years that had passed since it was written. When I looked up at Stanka she was handing me a package: "This also belongs to you."

Inside were two dresses, one blue and one white. Watching my bewildered face, Stanka explained: "You wore the blue doll's dress when Mom brought you home, and the white one, which we made out of a curtain, was for your baptism. There is also a notebook from when you learned to print the alphabet in the first grade."

As the day of my departure from Warsaw approached, I realized how my two-week visit had made me feel part of the family. Everyone was so warm and kind to me. They spoiled me in a way that no one had in a long time. It was an unforgettable event in my life. I was so fortunate to have found them and gotten to know them, and to have discovered what decent and marvelous people they were. But most of all, I was grateful to them for saving my life and unveiling the mystery of my early childhood.

Now that I knew I had been born in Radziwiłłów, Ukraine, I wanted to see that *shtetl* with my own eyes. I told Stanka about my wish. She said it would be too dangerous for a foreigner like me to travel there alone. She insisted that they accompany me there.

Before returning to Los Angeles, I stopped off in Tel Aviv, where I met with Yehuda Bornstein, the Koordynacja agent who had convinced the Roztropowiczes to return me to the Jewish people. I also had the opportunity to meet three other girls – Basia, Halinka, and Tami – whom he had brought to the orphanage at the same time as me. They all see each other in Israel on various occasions; I was the mystery person. It was fascinating to hear their stories. We took a picture identical to the one from Lodz, Poland some sixty years earlier.

When I returned home to Los Angeles, I started planning my next trip – my journey back to Radziwiłłów.

Tami Lavi, Halina Bernstein, Yehuda Bornstein, Basia David, and Sabina Heller,
above: Lodz, 1948; below: Tel Aviv, July, 2000

CHAPTER 27

Return to Radziwiłłów, 2002

fter getting to know my newly found family, my quest for identity and roots took me to Ukraine in 2002. The conditions there are very different from those to which we are accustomed in the West. Ukraine declared its independence from the Soviet Union in 1991. In the eyes of many Ukrainians, conditions deteriorated afterward because of government corruption. Poverty took on a new meaning, something I was to discover when I arrived.

I flew to Warsaw to meet Stanka and the rest of the family; Stanka organized the trip. We traveled by bus from Poland to Lviv, Ukraine. From there we took a taxi to Radziwiłłów. Zosia Stramska's brother Bolek accompanied us. He was an elderly gentleman, about eighty years old and very vivacious. He moved like a young man; nothing about him suggested his advanced age. He had written to his cousin Luba to inform her of our visit.

The road from Lviv to the Radziwiłłów prepared us for what was to come. As we neared the village, we were the only car on the road. Coming from Los Angeles, the city famous for congested freeways, it was very strange not to see any other vehicles on the road.

On one side of the street, people were selling mushrooms and wild blueberries they had collected in the woods. Others were selling home-baked goods. These were just housewives trying to make extra money, not commercial vendors.

We arrived in Radziwiłłów on my birthday, August 1. The sleepy little village consisted of single-family houses surrounded by vegetable gardens. Lovely colorful flowers proudly decorated the front of the houses. I could not help but notice wells in the yards of many of the houses. I thought they were very picturesque. In my innocence, I believed them to be some kind of beautiful décor for the yard. Soon I discovered that the wells served a more functional purpose – it was where the people got their water.

Radziwiłłów had few paved roads. Most of the streets were nothing more than dirt tracks. Ducks, chickens, dogs and cats strolled around the houses and onto the streets, blocking traffic at times. We were amazed to see so many horse-drawn carts. The roads were covered with puddles from the heavy rain of the previous night. You had to take care not to step into horse manure. The village reminded me of Anatevka, the fictional *shtetl* depicted in the musical *Fiddler on the Roof.*

At last we arrived at Luba's house and knocked on the door. We waited a few minutes; there was no answer. Bolek could not understand what had happened. He swore he had written to her advising her of the day and time of our arrival. He had not telephoned her, as long distance calls between Poland and Ukraine were very expensive. How could she have forgotten?

As he was about to check the back of the house, a short stout figure of a woman suspiciously opened the door a small crack. Her face was partially covered by her white scarf, revealing just a pair of blue eyes. She examined us out apprehensively, but when she noticed Bolek, she swung the door wide open and shrieked at the top of her voice, "Bolek, it's so good to see you!"

They embraced and Bolek introduced us. Luba apologized for keeping us waiting. She said she was expecting her son and grandson to return from the store. They were visiting her for a week.

She explained that she had never received Bolek's letter. A few moments later we discovered why. Bolek had included some cash with the letter. A post office employee must have stolen the money and discarded the letter.

We entered the house and found ourselves in a tiny kitchen. In fact, everything in that miniature kitchen was tiny. There was only enough room for one person. It had a small sink (the kind that you find in a bathroom) and a little table. From the kitchen, a door opened to the living room. The living room walls were covered with rugs used as tapestries. A vase with fresh-cut flowers decorated the table, and family photos were hanging on one wall and a picture of a Catholic saint on the other.

Luba's house had no indoor plumbing. People bathed out in the yard under the open sky. On a warm summer eve, that might be viewed as romantic, but I am certain that it was not much fun on a cold winter night.

Luba excused herself and left the kitchen, while Stanka and Bolek unpacked the gifts they had brought from Poland. Bolek had brought practically every basic food needed in a household – oil, bread, sugar and cheese – and Stanka had brought a variety of sausages, cold cuts, and candy.

Luba set the table for dinner. All the foods we had brought with us were there on the table. Luba added potatoes, tomatoes and cucumbers from her vegetable garden. Meat was rare and expensive.

I pointed out to Luba that there were no knives on the table. She whispered apologetically, in a low voice, "I don't have any knives. I sold them when we were broke, and never had enough money to buy new ones." Welcome to Ukraine.

While they were discussing the best way to obtain information about my biological parents, I looked around me. Luba's house was tiny. She would not be able to accommodate us. I was exhausted from our long journey from Poland, and then I had a flashback to our experience at the border crossing between Poland and Ukraine, where officials had collected the passports of all the passengers on the bus. They kept us waiting on the bus for about four hours, even though we were the only bus there. It seemed outrageous, and then Stanka explained that there was a lot of smuggling between Poland and Ukraine. Once in Lviv, we had to watch our wallets and our belongings closely. When I tried to use the public restrooms, I fled in disgust. They were two holes in the ground, and the odor was unbearable.

Secretly I was looking forward to a clean and comfortable hotel room, and I was ready to pay any price for that. I turned to Luba and brought the problem to her attention. I made it clear that I wanted to stay in a hotel overnight. Everybody started to laugh. I didn't understand what was so funny. She reassured me that we would manage, and insisted that we stay at her place. I kept insisting on the hotel. Finally, Luba gave in and said that there was only one hotel in town, and she knew a lady who worked there. Luba called her to make sure we were in good hands. Her friend reassured her that it was luxurious, so we decided to go there immediately.

Luba's son took us there in his car. As we approached the location of the hotel, we were met by a sorry sight – dirt roads, trash piled up everywhere, dilapidated buildings and decay all around us. The people I saw looked hopeless and desperate. Their clothes were old and ragged.

As I absorbed the atmosphere, our car came to a stop. We had arrived at the hotel. We entered an old building into what was supposed to be the lobby. It was dark and cold. We approached a receptionist. She was stern and mean-looking – a typical old Communist bureaucrat. After all paperwork was completed, we went to see the room. The room's lock was broken, it had two military cots, and everything looked dirty and shabby. When I sat on the cot, it sank down almost to the floor. The bare walls were covered with dirty spots. Some of the furniture was actually broken.

The bathroom was even worse. The plumbing was not inside the walls as in the West, and the pipes were rotting and moldy, which did not make for a pleasant sight. The tub was rusty and dirty. There was a vertical pipe that was seemingly the shower. When I turned it on, the water came down, one drop at a time. The place had not been swept or cleaned in a long time. Nobody came to apologize for the mess. Their attitude was: take it or leave it. We stayed because there was nowhere else to go.

To make matters worse, the hotel was located near a railroad station. It was a warm and humid summer night so we had to open the windows for ventilation. Then we turned off the lights and went to bed. I tossed and turned and couldn't fall asleep. I could hear the trains arriving in the station, squealing to a halt.

The sounds were familiar. In my mind I was taken back to the war. I felt cold sweat covering my body, and a great fear consuming me. Once again I experienced the terrible fear that was always lurking beneath the surface, of being alone and helpless in the darkness, hungry and abandoned. I could picture what my parents must have felt leaving their baby behind in the hands of strangers, feeling death hanging in the air. The enemy was waiting for them; there was no escape. It was probably the worst night in my adult life. I finally fell asleep at dawn.

I awoke very early, relieved it was daytime. Somehow things seemed better in the morning. It was symbolic that I had come back to my birthplace on my birthday. It was as if my life had come full circle. I was convinced it was a good sign. My wish, of course, was to find some information about my biological parents, the Kagans, but it was not to be.

The Mayor's Office

Luba's son knew the purpose of my trip to Radziwiłłów. The mayor of Radziwiłłów was his high-school friend, and he arranged for me to meet the mayor that morning. I had high hopes. Radziwiłłów was where it had all happened. If any information existed, it should have been right there.

I had heard how difficult it was to get information from any office in Ukraine. In addition to the language barrier, there corruption was rife – you needed to bribe government officials in order to get anything done. I felt lucky to have access to the mayor, thanks to Stanka's connections. The mayor's office was in a small, old building. All signs were in Ukrainian. As we entered the building, we immediately found ourselves in a large waiting room. The old wooden floors creaked with every step we took. We sat down, waiting for the secretary to call us.

Luba's daughter and son told us about the difficulties they encountered daily. Her daughter described how the previous year she had taken ill and needed emergency surgery. She was relatively lucky because she had a job working in a delicatessen owned by the mayor.

She told me that the government does not provide health insurance. "We are on our own. You have to pay for any health service or surgery in cash. I am lucky my family collected the money for my surgery," she informed us. "Not only that, but my co-workers took on my workload so I wouldn't lose my job."

The mayor's secretary then asked us into the mayor's office. It was a large room, surprisingly cool compared to the temperature outside. There was an odor of decay typical to very old buildings. A desk, the mayor's armchair, and two chairs for visitors were the only furniture. As we approached, I could not help but notice the lack of computers, and the remarkable neatness of the mayor's desk. There was not the usual clutter of papers you might encounter in a modern, Western government office. Everything was very simple.

The mayor rose to greet us. He was a man in his forties, dressed in a black suit, and had dark hair and brown eyes. He looked Middle Eastern. I found out later that he was of Armenian descent. Both Ukrainian and Polish societies are homogenous, which made the fact that Radziwiłłów had an Armenian mayor very surprising.

The mayor greeted us with a warm smile, and made me feel at ease.

"Sorry to keep you waiting, but my secretary went down to the archives to look for information on the war years," he said.

I felt my heart pounding. It was the moment I had been waiting for. Who knew what I may find? Finally the secretary returned with a large notebook in her hands. She handed it to the mayor. The mayor turned the pages slowly, scanning each page. I could see handwritten names. He went through the entire notebook and repeated the process with the few other notebooks from the war.

At last he turned to us and said, "I am afraid I don't have what you are looking for. The books we have in our archives contain records only of Ukrainian citizens of the Orthodox religion. Until 1945, marriage and birth certificates were the property of each religious institute. The Catholic Church kept records of their members, and the Jewish synagogue kept records of members of their faith. Since the Nazis burned the synagogue, we must assume that the records were burned as well. Somebody may have managed to hide and transfer the records to a safer place, but it is very unlikely."

So I was back where I had started, back to square one.

"If you like, I will take you to the site where the Nazis killed the 3,000 Jews of Radziwiłłów," the mayor offered. We accepted, and the mayor took us in his car to the location of the mass murder, some three kilometers out of the city. On the way he told us he was too young to remember, but his grandmother was a witness to what had happened that day.

The Jews were ordered to assemble in the main town square. From there, the men women, children and the elderly were ordered to walk three kilometers. Huge pits had already been dug. They were ordered to stand around the pits. Then the Germans shot them and they fell into the pits. The mass graves were then covered with dirt to erase all traces of these atrocious murders. When the Soviets liberated Ukraine, they planted trees on top of the mass graves, turning them into a wooded area.

As I walked through the woods, I found a sign indicating that the area was a huge cemetery. I noticed lots of ants crawling around, common when bodies are not embalmed or placed in protective caskets. A few stairs led to a simple stone situated on a small slope erected in memory of the victims. The text on the memorial stone read: "Here, the Nazis murdered 3,000 citizens of Radziwiłłów." Not one word mentioned the crucial fact that all of the victims were Jews.

Only one Jewish family still lived in Radziwiłłów, and the mayor introduced me to them. I told the family of my disappointment at the stone set by the communists at the site where the Radziwiłłów Jews had been murdered. To my surprise, they said that Israel was in the process of erecting a beautiful monument at the site, which would make it clear that all the victims were Jews.

As we walked back to the car, the mayor spoke, as if reading our minds. He said that many Ukrainians regarded the horrible fate of the Jews as a foreshadowing of their own future fate. The lyrics of a popular song at that time said, "The Germans have come – *gut*; for the Jews – *kaput* (bad); for the Gypsies – *tosze* [as well]; for the Ukrainians – *posze* [later]." The mayor also mentioned another popular wartime saying: "The Jews are used instead of water to make the dough; the Ukrainians will be used instead of yeast to knead the dough."

I was very sad that I could not identify the exact location of the grave of my biological parents. Deep in my heart I thought how very lucky I was that my destiny had taken me out of there. Even though the war was over, the shadows of the past still lingered there. It was a gloomy, depressing place. Not much had changed since the war. Progress had never reached that tiny, forsaken village.

There my feelings of safety left me. That was where I had been abused, neglected and abandoned. All I was left with was fear, the fear that had accompanied me all my life.

Psychological, clinical and even animal research all confirm the enormous impact of trauma on the young mind and the critical importance of experiences in the earliest years of life, as well as the consequences they may have later in adult life. This must explain my frequent inner feelings of dark emptiness and dull sadness, even though I appear to be a normal adult on the outside. Appearances can be deceiving.

In college, I used to be jealous of my friends who were so happy, cheerful and self-confident, talking and laughing, raising their hands in class to debate an argument. I, on the other hand, sat quietly, self-conscious and reserved. I could never be that happy and carefree. There was always a cloud hanging over me.

I remember my mother saying to me when I was growing up, "You should be more assertive with people. You have everything going for you. What is holding you back?"

I had no explanation as to why I felt the way I did. But now I found that all this time Radziwiłłów had held the key to my adult behavior. My birthplace will always be associated in my mind with abuse, fear, the lack of a sense of security and abandonment. All of these were deciding factors in the way I developed as an adult. The link to my dark past was still there, just beneath the surface.

The mayor's car coming to a halt brought me back to reality. My hopes that he would be able to solve the mystery of my biological parents' identity never materialized. However, even though my trip to Radziwiłłów had not revealed anything new about the Kagans, it had helped me understand things about myself.

I returned with Stanka and Bolek to Poland, and from there I flew home to Los Angeles.

CHAPTER 28

Reflections

Natalia's letter, Stanka's stories and Zosia Stramska's memories of me from when I was hidden in that cellar had all shed new light on some of my behavior. I suddenly remembered an incident from when I was perhaps nine years old, living with my parents in our own apartment on 11 Sprinzak Street (name changed from Bikurei Hitim) in Tel Aviv. A few months earlier, the Weintal family had moved in next door to us. They were patients of my mother and had a son named Danny who was exactly my age. He was also an only child like me. Danny and I became best friends. We spent many hours playing together in each other's homes.

One afternoon, I was returning from the seamstress who was sewing a dress for me from the fabric of my mother's old dress. We did not have enough money to buy new fabric. The seamstress' shop was not far from our apartment. It was winter and already dark. I was walking fast, anxious to get home; I knew I would be coming into a dark, empty house. There would be nobody home as my mother was at work and my father at a coffee shop with his buddies. Suddenly I felt somebody following me. I heard his footsteps clearly behind me. I was scared. I could feel my heart beating fast. I started to walk even faster. The person behind me increased his speed as well, to keep up with me. I could already see my house. I became panicky and decided to run. I could hear the person following me start running as well. I was almost home. I screamed as loud as I could.

All the neighbors came out onto their balconies. My friend Danny and his parents came downstairs. They asked me what had happened. I told them somebody was chasing me, and I was afraid. They checked the neighborhood. They found no one. Danny's parents took me up to their apartment and calmed me down. His mother prepared supper for me. I started to feel better, feeling safe again. When my parents returned home, they found out what had happened.

Often I question how much my parents knew about what had happened to me before they adopted me. They used to leave me alone all the time. Didn't they realize how traumatized I must have been by my horrible experience in that dark cellar? Yes, they needed to work. Life in Israel was difficult. But all the neighbors knew I was always at home alone. I was alone even when most people returned home from work. What I did not understand then and maybe I am learning now, is that it took us many years to bond as a family. As painful as those years were, they were my normal years, the good years.

Of course, now I have a fairly good understanding of the source of my fear of darkness. My prolonged stay in the dark, cold cellar as an infant apparently caused me to react in such extreme ways whenever I found myself in darkness again, even many years later. This sense of overwhelming fear would take hold of me; it was a hysterical reaction that I am still unable to control.

My son Mark said to me one day: "Mom you're always afraid. How can you live like that?"

I don't like to live in fear. I fight it every day. Most of the time I win, and sometimes I lose. My fears do not paralyze me. They are subdued; they lay dormant, deep down inside me, lurking and waiting to come out whenever I am not in control. For example, one night I mistakenly took a wrong turn while driving on a freeway in Los Angeles. I became hysterical and began crying and screaming. My body broke out into a cold sweat. I could not think straight. I was convinced that I was lost and would never return home. Again, I was alone in the dark – helpless and forgotten. Of course, if I had been thinking logically, all I had to do was simply exit the freeway, pull into a gas station and ask for directions. But fear sometimes makes us irrational.

Some of the ways that I have learned to fight fear is always to be on alert, to have a plan, and never to be caught by surprise. I try to be aware of my surroundings, and how to survive if anything happens. When I am sitting in a restaurant, I always check where the exit is. My chair is not pushed all the way forward – I leave it at a slight angle for a quick escape.

I read the documents from the Jewish Historical Institute in Warsaw over and over. I know them by heart. I am beginning to get acquainted with the new part of me – the part that has been missing for all those years. It was quite painful to read about the abuse and neglect by the Miszczak family. But when I read about my rescue, the Roztropowicz family restored my faith in the goodness of humankind.

The Koordynacja had required Natalia Roztropowicz to bring me in person to the Jewish orphanage in Lodz. They advised her to drop me off without any explanation, and then disappear.

I know from the letters that I wrote to Natalia from the orphanage that I loved her very much. I know from Natalia's letter how very traumatic and painful the decision to give me up was for her. She experienced the pain of a mother's separation from her child. That separation must have affected me deeply, too.

As I now understand it, I was too young to understand my feelings when all that was happening to me. I was in a daze and confused. I did not cry, nor was I sad, as I should have been. Facing the separation would have been too excruciating, so I suppressed my feelings. It was my way of protecting myself from the horrible hurt. It was my defense mechanism in action. On the surface I looked like a happy child, but underneath was a very frightened little girl.

Now when I read about it, I am infuriated. I was never given a chance or encouraged to talk about my feelings. I was just expected to go on with life as though nothing had happened. It is frustrating to read how poorly informed and insensitive the Koordynacja was with regard to the children's well being.

As Natalia's daughter, I felt betrayed once more by the very people I trusted and loved. At first, I did not realize it was final. I thought I was at the orphanage just for the summer. But as time passed, I realized that the Roztropowicz family was out of my life forever. That is when it became unbearable. What could I do? I was a little girl at the mercy of the adults around me.

Today, I have shared with my co-workers and neighbor some of my discoveries about my past. My colleagues, with whom I have worked for many years, were surprised to discover my amazing past.

I remember an incident, right after I received the documents, when my neighbor Carol dropped in for a chat. I asked her to come with me to the kitchen, where I was preparing dinner.

Carol said, "What's the matter? Is everything ok? You look upset."

I turned to her and answered, "How would you feel if you discovered you were adopted, and your parents had never told you anything about it? Everybody in Israel knew about my adoption except me."

I felt the rage building up in me as I spoke. Carol looked surprised at my display of anger. She sat there for what felt like a long time, seeming almost annoyed. At last she said:

> I, for one, can understand your parents' position very well. As a person who adopted a child, I can identify with their dilemma. They were fearful of losing you and your love for them. I see why they would be hesitant to tell you the truth. They probably were waiting for the right moment. They were anxious to protect you from the horrors of your childhood.

This irritated me further. Why did she fail to see that her situation was so different from my parents'?

"Carol, the Kagans were already dead. My parents had nothing to worry about. I was not going anywhere. I could accept the argument that they were waiting for me to grow up, so that I could deal with it better. But they went to their graves with that secret. They denied me the right to the truth. I find it hard to forgive them."

Carol remained doubtful. "I met Zygmund and Sophia. They loved you very much. They were good people. Whatever they did, they had your best interests at heart."

She showed no empathy for me. I felt like a victim. "Why can't you show any consideration for how I feel?" I asked.

Carol was not moved. "I just understand where your parents were coming from." Then she excused herself to go to work and came over to me, gave me a hug and left. From that moment on I decided to keep my inner feelings to myself.

My friends might have been right, but I found no comfort in their interpretations. I was furious and hurt. I needed to grieve for the loss of the Kagans, whom I did not remember at all. I wanted to mourn the loss of love and care, as well as my childhood. I needed time to grieve for the loss of the old *me*.

Adaptation

Hidden children are very good at adapting to new situations. Adapting meant the difference between life and death.

It always took a great deal of effort to fit in wherever I lived, whether with the Roztropowiczes, or with Sophia and Zygmund Goszczewski in Poland, in Israel, or in the US with my husband. I was the one who had to make that extra effort regarding things that to other people were ordinary. I hated being singled out as different. My instinct was to adjust.

I disliked riding on the bus in Tel Aviv with my mother. She would always speak to me in Polish, and everyone on the bus would stare at us. I felt awkward and insecure in the spotlight. My idea of comfort is to blend in, never to be singled out.

I *thought* I had succeeded.

While I was reading the documents regarding my childhood, I realized two astonishing facts:

1) I, who all my life tried to distance myself from the survivors' generation, found out that I was a survivor;
2) I, who tried so hard to fit in, felt that I did not really fit in anywhere.

Even though I am a survivor I do not really fit with the survivors. Most of them have memories of their families and the happy times before the war, as well as memories of the horrors of the ghetto and the camps. I don't. I remember clearly only from the age of eight. I have no concrete memories prior to that age.

Most survivors are older than I. Many seem to be in pain all the time, remembering their tragic experiences during the Holocaust, with which they are often preoccupied. Many such people have a victim mentality.

I thought that I was different. My upbringing in Israel helped me to be more active than passive. Growing up with Holocaust survivors made me want to be strong and self-reliant. I refused to be a victim.

CHAPTER 29

Healing

In Los Angeles, it is widely accepted that everyone goes to therapy. I decided to go to therapy, too. In my therapy sessions, I tried to peel off the layers of the past and discover who I was.

In January 2003, the late psychologist Dan Bar-On, a professor at Ben Gurion University, gave the keynote lecture at a conference at the Imperial War Museum in London entitled "Beyond the Camps and Forced Labor." The conference brought together scholars from various fields that research different groups of survivors of Nazi persecution. In his talk Professor Bar-On said: "You have to learn to cry when you mourn the loss of what will never return." I felt I was never given an opportunity to mourn or cry.

At first, I was abandoned and starved. I stopped crying. Stanka describes in her diary how *they had to teach me how to cry* after they rescued me from the cellar. As an older child, I was passed from hand to hand without any explanation. No one gave me the chance to grieve the loss of a family and a happy childhood. Only now have I begun to learn how to cry, which is helping me in my healing process.

I discussed this in therapy. I feel that even though I lack the exact facts of my Holocaust experiences, my past has had enormous consequences on my adult life. As I was reflecting on the different periods in my life, I began to understand behaviors that were previously incomprehensible to me. Some episodes in my life started to take on a new meaning, such as the time that I asked my mother Sophia, "Who do you love more, Dad or me?"

This is a common question many children ask their parents. I could never understand her answer: "I love Dad more because I've known him longer."

I am beginning to understand it now. At that time we were just bonding as a family. She did not have much experience as a mother. She probably did not even realize what a terrible answer that was. I was looking for a confirmation of love. Her answer was very painful for me. It was so hurtful that I remember it until today. I am not sure there is a way to eliminate the pain completely.

I remember when Zygmund and Sophia came to visit me when I had my first child, Ron. I had no idea how to care for the baby. My husband and I took classes at the Red Cross. It was helpful but not enough. I had a difficult delivery with some complications. I needed help at home with the baby. It was comforting to know that Mom was there with me. She would help and guide me. After all, she was a doctor.

I had brought up my concerns to my mother before going to the hospital. She seemed a little bothered and apprehensive. She said she would discuss the matter with my father. The next morning she looked more relaxed. She approached Alfred and me and said: "We don't want you to worry about caring for the baby. We want you to hire a nurse. We will be happy to pay."

I was somewhat disappointed, but I accepted, not giving it much thought. I could not understand why *she* would not want to help me care for her first grandson. It was strange. A few years later, Alfred and I went to Israel to visit my parents, this time with both children. They were so happy we were coming with their grandchildren. They could not wait to show them off to their friends and relatives. It was a happy time, but it was marred by one incident.

One afternoon, I wanted to have some time alone with Alfred. I turned to my mother and asked her if she would you mind staying with the children for a couple of hours, so that we could go out and have some time alone.

"No, I am afraid I can't. I don't think I can handle two small children. Maybe you should leave them when Tamara [the housekeeper] is here.")

Her answer infuriated me. I thought to myself, "What kind of grandma are you? You are the only grandma that refuses to babysit her grandchildren. Any grandma would be delighted to spend time with her grandchildren, especially when they come for a visit from so far away." I couldn't comprehend her attitude. I left the room without saying another word.

I wondered how I was going to explain my mother's strange behavior to my husband. I felt embarrassed. Why was she being so selfish? What was wrong with her?

Luckily, Tamara agreed to stay with Ron and Mark. Soon I forgot all about it. I attributed her behavior to the fact that she was so involved in her career that she had no patience for anything else. Now I can understand her fear of being alone with the children. She had no experience dealing with infants or toddlers. They adopted me when I was six years old. She did not want to give away her secret that she had never taken care of babies. She didn't want to fail as a grandma. I wish she were here so I could tell her she was not a bad grandma. I wish she had told me the truth. Things would have been easier for both of us.

In 2002, I attended the International Child Survivors Conference in Toronto. I discovered that many survivors had gone into care-giving professions. I was not unique. Maybe I decided to become a teacher because I had been a frightened child, alone in a cellar. I wanted to help other children. I understand my pupils – children of immigrants from Mexico who are left alone when their parents work. I experienced it first hand. The hours spent in school were the best time of their day. I try to create a pleasant learning environment for them.

During the conference, the question of how best to deal with the discoveries of my past came to mind. Should I dwell on the past and build my life around these findings? Now that I know my past, do I dedicate my life to that memory and put the present aside, or do I go on with my life as before?

A curator from the US Holocaust Memorial Museum in Washington D.C. was collecting artifacts from child survivors for the opening of an exhibit about the Hidden Children named, "Life in Shadows." I donated Stanka's original diary, my blue doll's dress and some photos.

In 2003 Mark accompanied me to the Child Survivor's Conference in Washington, and at the same time we went to see "Life in Shadows" at the Museum. It was his way of supporting me in the discovery of my past. My participation in the exhibit landed my child survivor's story on the first page of the *Los Angeles Daily News*.

I now know that I lost my happy childhood when the Kagans perished. That loss can never be regained. Thanks to pure coincidence, I was able to reconnect with the surviving Roztropowiczes and learn from them about the identity they gave me during the five years I lived with them.

Then in the orphanage I discovered I was actually a Jewish orphan. A few months later Zygmund and Sophia Goszczewski adopted me, becoming the only parents I ever knew. I went through anger, frustration and, finally, acceptance. I am coming to terms with the different stages of my past. After reading Natalia's letter, I feel grateful to her for making the decision that saved my life, and I forgive her for the way she dropped me at the orphanage. I realize she was advised by the Jewish Coordination to do so.

I feel frustrated with the Jewish Coordination's insensitive behavior and the psychologically damaging way they treated us, the children. I was upset with my parents for severing all ties with the Roztropowicz family, and saddened by the Coordination for not keeping their promise to Natalia to inform her of my whereabouts.

Nevertheless, I have deep love and admiration for Zygmund and Sophia. They chose me when most adoptive parents would have preferred a baby, and gave me a loving, stable home. I forgive them for any mistakes they made knowingly or unknowingly. They are my parents and they always will be.

I have had a chance to think about what would have happened had I stayed with the Roztropowicz family. After talking to the surviving Roztropowiczes, I discovered that Natalia passed away five years after she took me to the orphanage. Józef remarried shortly after her death. The Roztropowicz children were grown up by that time and had moved out. I, however, would have still been a minor and would have ended up with another mother. Would she have loved me? I really don't know. So, I feel that whatever happened was for a purpose, and this realization makes it easier for me to accept my fate.

Indeed, I feel fortunate. A million-and-a-half Jewish children babies did not survive. I did. Moreover, I have been blessed with people who loved me and parents who made every effort and every sacrifice to help me become who I am now.

In spite of the darkness of the Holocaust, I turned out to be a good person. I still believe that human beings are basically good, and I am optimistic about the future. By embracing the past and my various identities, I am slowly emerging from the darkness.

Inka Kagan
Irena Roztropowicz
Ina Goszczewski
Sabina Heller
Encino, California 2008

EPILOGUE

My life story concludes with an unpredictable surprise, when, after forty years, I reunited with Avram, my love from my youth. Avram was the one who asked me how I knew that my parents were my real parents.

One afternoon, after my son Ron brought me my mail, I became irritated when I saw the number of bills I had to pay. I was about to toss all those envelopes onto my desk, when a letter from Israel caught my attention. I looked to see who the sender was and found that it was from Avram. I almost fell off the chair. We had split up when he went on to study in Cambridge, England, and I ended up getting married and had moved to the United States. I felt a sharp pain in my chest just seeing his name. It brought back a rush of feelings that I had managed very well to bury as deep as I could for so many years.

He came back into my life when I least expected; it was a great gift for the coming new year. I feel that even in my wildest dreams I could not have asked for a more wonderful way to conclude my life story. My reunion with Avram brought new hope and made life beautiful and worth living.

APPENDIX 1

The Rescue of Inka Kagan

Natalia Roztropowicz with her wartime
daughter, Inka Kagan, Nidzica, 1945

A letter written by Natalia Roztropowicz

This letter was written in 1947. Inka received it fifty-three years later, at a ceremony honoring Józef and Natalia Roztropowicz as Righteous Among the Nations.

– "A Mother Given by God" –
Hoping it will reach Inka, her adopted daughter

December 19, 1947

For a long time I have been meaning to write what I am writing now. This is the tragic life story of our youngest daughter – Inka. I don't know if God wanted it this way, or if it was a divine test. Certainly, it was an extremely difficult and dangerous test for my family, and for me. For this one-and-a-half-year-old baby we risked our lives, and that of three of our own children. Our oldest daughter Zosia had been taken to forced labor [in Germany] by the Germans, our enemy. We prayed for her life constantly. Maybe our risky decision to shelter Inka would spare Zosia's life. I didn't know. We did what good Christians should do; whether we did the right thing or not, God alone will judge.

That winter and summer of 1943, we could not sleep at the farmhouse; we feared for our lives at the hands of the Ukrainians. We were the last ones to leave our farm, located on the outskirts of town. In June 1943 we were finally forced to pack up and vacate the farm, leaving for the Ukrainian village of Radziwiłłów. All the Poles left the farm. The Ukrainians viciously murdered whoever stayed. We moved in with a teacher named Karczem, sharing his living quarters on the Krupska Highway. He soon fled, but we remained.

I cannot guarantee the accuracy of the events I am going to describe – it was what the people in our town said. I am not going to mention names. The condition in which we found the child seems to confirm those rumors.

I'd like to go back to when I first learned about Inka. This part I can swear is true.

In July, rumors circulated about a Jewish baby hidden in horribly inhumane conditions in the adjacent house. Locked up in a dark cellar, she was maltreated and starving. How did this happen?

A Polish policeman named Miszczak (along with his wife and two daughters) who lived 12 kilometers from our farm had given shelter to the Kagans, a young, Jewish, married couple. They had a precious baby girl named Inka. We heard about Inka while still living on our farm. We did not know the Miszczaks personally, but they had a bad reputation. The policeman kept the young couple for a while, and then kicked them out. The baby stayed with the policeman's family. The Kagan parents inquired about the fate of their child through the people who lived in the village. Sadly, we never knew them.

After the last raid on the Radziwiłłów ghetto, we were asked to inquire whether the baby was still there. I could not do it because I had to cross a field, and such a long walk was very dangerous for a Pole to do alone.

At the beginning of July, we found out that our new next-door-neighbors were the infamous Miszczak couple hiding Inka. They had escaped from their farmhouse to our city of Radziwiłłów. We could not help Inka, the innocent infant, because German soldiers lived in our apartment. All they had left us was one room and a kitchen. The rest of the house served as the headquarters for the German Air Force. The Germans filled our yard with barracks. To talk about the child publicly would have meant a death sentence for her. But the appalling conditions in which the baby existed may have been worse than death. Oh, what could we do?

At the end of July, Mrs. Miszczak and her two children (now young adults) moved to the nearby city of Brody, Ukraine near Radziwiłłów. Like the rest of the Poles, they needed to escape from the Ukrainian Nationalists, who threatened to massacre them. Mr. Miszczak stayed behind. He was the only one who was kind to Inka. But he worked at a police station, sometimes staying away from home for 48-hour shifts, and had no time to care for Inka. Inka was left all alone in the dark, cold cellar. The policemen's family used to go away for three nights a week to the neighboring town of Radziwiłłów. They left baby Inka behind alone in the farmhouse for days without food or heat. Fortunately for Inka, nobody broke into farmhouse or burned it when they were away. Three days later, they would come back from Radziwiłłów and find the house intact and, miraculously, Inka still alive. Finally, they stayed in Radziwiłłów. They locked her in the cellar; they didn't know any other safe way of getting rid of her.

After the policeman's wife and children took off permanently for Brody, people began talking about the condition of the child, and where she was. I didn't believe the stories, and wanted to see the child for myself.

A few days later Zosia Stramska – a young girl who lived next door to the abandoned child and used to sneak in and feed Inka, came over to our house and told me to follow her. She was going to show me Inka's hiding place.

All of a sudden, Milka, one of the policeman's daughters, arrived at the house. Zosia whispered, "I will keep Milka with the Germans in a room far from the cellar. While she is there, I'll let you into the kitchen, which leads to the cellar where the child is." My daughters Jana and Stanka entered the kitchen on tiptoe. There was a little door near the stove. Zosia opened the door slowly.

For as long as I live, I will never forget what I saw. I am pretty tough, but the vision sent shockwaves through my entire body. I saw a corpse; her hair standing on end, her eyes bulging, her neck like a thin stick, and her hands with long nails that curled upwards. She looked like a skeleton. She hardly moved. She was sitting in a small wooden cradle, in the bottom of which were holes covered with straw. The urine ran down to the floor through the holes, while the excrement remained on the straw.

When a ray of light entered through the open door, she did not blink her eyes, but something moved – maybe I imagined it, but it seemed she called "Mama!" Maybe it was my imagination, because she did not know how to talk yet. In any case, we decided then and there to take her with us. I could feel her breath as I cradled her under my coat.

We consulted with my husband Józef, our children Andrzej [Jendryk], Stanka and Jana, and our oldest daughter, Zosia. We debated long and hard about what to do with Inka! After a serious family meeting, we decided to keep the little baby as our own. We knew that to take her in would be a huge risk for our entire family, but to leave her there alone to die from hunger? – we could not. If we went to the Gestapo, they'd shoot her; we did not have that right. This was a human being – a baby who had not harmed anybody. We would not stain our hands with innocent blood. My husband made the final decision to take the child into our family.

I thought to myself, "Maybe thanks to our act of kindness, my daughter Zosia will come across good people in Germany who will take care of her." And that is exactly what happened. A Catholic priest looked after Zosia in Germany for the entire winter as if she were family.

In the spring, Zosia had to return to work in Germany, but the priest continued to look after her as much as he could. God's blessing was with her.

After we decided to take Inka in, I went to our priest and he told me he would do whatever he could to help. But our decision was our own responsibility. He provided us with a document stating that we now had five children, including our oldest daughter Zosia in Germany; our now youngest daughter Irena (Inka) was two years old.

While my husband and our daughters stayed at home, my thirteen-year-old son Jendryk and I went to the militia in Brody, where Mr. Miszczak worked. I told him that since his wife and daughters had left, there was no one to care for Inka. I asked him to give her to us. He was shocked. After he regained his composure, he said, "Do you realize we cannot talk about this child?"

I answered, "I know. It is our personal problem."

He said, "You go home. I will go a different way. I will meet you at my house and give you the child."

Jendryk raced home to tell the girls to heat water for a bath and warm up some milk. I went straight to Miszczak's house.

The policeman pulled her out of her hiding place like a cat, holding her by her gown. Then his conscience began to bother him, and he said, "My girls neglected the child, and I am too busy at work."

I took her under my coat, not even looking at her. I only felt she was still alive.

As I was walking home, a terrible fear overcame me. I thought, "God, what will happen if the child has typical Jewish features? What will happen to our children?" But it was too late to back out.

When I got home, the water in the tub was warm and the milk ready in a bottle. I gently put her in the water. She started to rock her body back and forth the way we saw her doing in hiding. Her back was one layer of waste. We took her out of the tub, dried her off and dressed her in a dress that we took off one of our daughter's dolls. The doll's clothes were the only things that would fit her tiny body. She was one month short of two years.

I took her into the dining room and set her down on the sofa as a new member of the family. When we turned on the lights, we were stunned at how skinny she was – just skin and bones hanging like little bags. Her neck was long and very thin; her round head full of curly blonde locks; dark eyebrows; big, bulging blue eyes. Her tongue was full of sores from sucking. She was very scared and, for a long time, she moved only her eyes. She kept still, not moving her head, like she was afraid of a hat dropping off. She didn't cry; she just turned pale and started to shake.

We gave her some milk diluted with water. We worried she might have an intestinal spasm as she had not eaten anything in a long time.

The first time she screamed was when the policeman's family came to visit us. They said they were very concerned that Inka might have tuberculosis. That was why she looked so awful. The policeman's wife said that Inka had no clothes except for two torn dresses, a pair of white shoes and a little purple blanket. We washed all her belongings. Their visit was the first time Inka screamed fearfully and grasped my neck tightly. However, when the policeman approached her, she ran into his arms cheerfully. From that, I figured out that he was the only one who had treated her kindly, like a human being.

In contrast, when his daughter approached her, bringing a jar of jam, Inka turned pale and started shaking.

As the time went by, Inka began to recover and rapidly regain her health. I gave her a lot of milk and vegetable soup. She would eat the carrots, parsley and onions out of the soup. When she took a bite of bread, she would say "ahh," as if it was the sweetest thing she had ever tasted.

It became a household expression: "If you aren't hungry, look how Inka eats and your appetite will soon return!"

Inka's bladder was still not healthy. She urinated non-stop. We put hot packs and hot water bottles on her at night. Then she got a rash all over her body, followed by boils filled with pus. The doctor informed us that it was her metabolism. Her body had been shutting down, dying, and now it was coming back to life. We kept her in the sun for hours.

Our daughters were living at home, hiding so that they would not be sent to Germany. But we decided not to hide Inka. On the contrary, I carried her in my arms wherever I went – going downtown, feeding the cows in the field – telling everyone that we took her sick from a wagon of Poles escaping their farms on the way to Radziwiłłów and later to Galicia, because it was more peaceful there. This story was credible.

When in March 1944 the Red Army entered Radziwiłłów and we had miraculously survived, we told the first Jew, named Bojm, to try to find Inka's parents or family. Unfortunately, her parents had perished. The Ukrainians had burned their shelter under a stable belonging to a Pole whose name I cannot remember. All her relatives had been killed as well. So we kept Inka, bringing her to Nidzica. She was officially baptized on July 15, 1945. I told the Russians what had happened, and they issued us a certificate declaring Inka as Irena Roztropowicz, our daughter.

Some Jews came by wanting to take her away, treating the matter in a very business-like manner. We said no. We wanted to guarantee that her future would be a happy one. The Jewish Committee from Bytom issued papers confirming that Inka was Jewish, and that we did not take her in for any profit. During that entire time, I only met a few Jews who understood the real reason why we did not want give her up. Giving her up would have been very hard on us, because we loved her like our own child. We went through a lot for her. But on the other hand, if we kept her, we were afraid that in the future it might backfire on us, because when she found out who she really was she might become angry at us for keeping her out of personal feelings. We could give her no more than our home and our love.

The Jewish Committee [Koordynacja] promised us mountains of gold in return for Inka. I went to talk to the Committee a few times – it was a long and difficult journey. These were tough times for us, after the war. We had a big family to feed. But we would not take charity from anybody. God delivered her into our hands, and I hoped that everything would work out well for her.

So I reach the end of Inka's story. I write this letter for her. When I think how I had to let her go, it upsets me terribly. But at the same time, I'm afraid that life would have been hard for her in our community, though in our home we would always have surrounded her with love and care.

The time has come to part with you, Inuś. Beloved Inka, do not hold it against us that we let you go! We did not do it for monetary gain, but because reason dictated it so. Dear child, maybe one day you will be able to understand and appreciate this act. This must be the hardest decision of my life. I don't know how I will survive. I had to take you to the orphanage myself and leave you there. Inuś, please understand that this was for your own good! Don't forget us. Don't believe anybody who says bad things about us, because letting you go was a big sacrifice for me.

Your fellow Jews could have given us money for your upbringing, but they didn't want to. We could not offer you anything but our love.

Someday maybe we will see each other again. Remember child – as your mother was given to you from God – keep God in your heart, and don't forget that you were baptized. Pray, and God will give you a good life. Forgive me again for any pain I have caused you.

Your mother,

Natalia Roztropowicz

Translated from the Polish by Sabina Heller

Natalia Roztropowicz's original letter to Inka

The English translation includes brief sections from additional material
that Natalia had written for Inka.

Dawno już miałam   19 3/XII/45.
zamiar opisać to, co Niusia
obecnie pisze, a jest to smutna i
tragiczna historja córeczki naszej,
najmłodszej – Niusi!
Nie wiem, czy to Bóg tak chciał,
czy to była próba dla nas, a
ciężka to była i niebezpieczna
próba – bo dla tego 1½ go
maleństwa – życiowskiego pochodze...
uważaliśmy życie 3ga swoich
własnych, w rozkwicie młodości
dzieci, no i swoje własne.
Ale nasza Lodzia, była sama-
samiutka tam u Niemców, a
wrogów, a taka młoda, każdej
chwili groziła jej śmierć!
Może więc tam uczynkiem
uratowaliśmy jej życie! Nie
wiem nic! – wiem to tylko, że

zrobiliśmy to, co powinien był zrobić
każdy Chrześcianin! Czy dobrze –
czy źle – niech Bóg osądzi!!

Gdy w 1943 roku w czerwcu
zmuszeni byliśmy opuścić nasze
gospodarstwo i przenieść się
do miasta Radziwiłłowa k/Brodów
bo już nikogo z Polaków na wsi nie
pozostało, kto w czas nie uciekł
został w bestialski sposób zamor-
dowany przez Ukraińców. Zostaliśmy
a naszej placówki ostatni!
Zamieszkaliśmy razem z nauczycie...
p. Karczem w jego mieszkaniu
po Krupieckiej szosie. Oni
wpierwszce wyjechali, a my
pozostaliśmy w ich mieszkaniu
W lipcu wczesną się wiadomość
naturalnie szeptana, że w sąsiedn...

domu, koło nas, przechowywuje się żydowskie
dziecko, jest w okropnem stanie,
wprost maltretowane, bite, żydowskie
i zamknięte w ciemnej komórce!
O tem, że ci ludzie, mieszkający
przedtem na wsi, wzięli na
przechowanie rodzinę żydowską,
składającą się z młodego małżeństwa
i ich malutkiej córeczki, dowiedzieliśmy
jeszcze będąc u siebie na gospodarce
nie znaliśmy ich osobiście, bo nie
cieszyli się zbyt dobrą opinją,
i mieszkali od nas o 12 kil.
dowodż po ostatniej akcyi
żydowskiej, nazwisk nie wymieniano,
proponowano mnie, abym dowiedziała
się czy to chłodzie tam żyją!
Nie mogłam tego zrobić bo
w te czasy iść przez pola samej,
polce, taki kawał drogi, było
niebezpiecznie!

I tak – w początku lipca los zdarzył
że zamieszkaliśmy obok domu,
w którym mieszkała ta rodzina,
uciekając ze wsi do miasta!
Pomóc temu maleństwu
nie można było, – w domu u nas
pełno mieńców, powoli zostawili
nam jeden pokoik i kuchnię, a
cały dom zajęli pod sztab
łotewkowy, na podwórku – baraki
z mieńcami. Zrobić wszędzie – to
skazać maleństwo na śmierć!
Warunki w jakich egzystowało
może były i gorsze od śmierci!
Co robić?! W końcu lipca cała
ta szanowna rodzina, składająca
się z matki i trojga, prawie dorosłych
dzieci, wyjścia do Brodów, jak
i większość polaków, ratując życie
przed ukraińcami, porostają

tylko ojciec (on jeden odnosił się do dziecka
po ludzku) ; to maleństwo znikając?
w ciemnej komórce. On pracuje
w policyi, więc nieraz całą i więcej
nie'ma go w domu – a dziecko ? –
Do tego miesiąca lipca 1943 roku
gdy los oprowadził nasze drogi,
historja dziecka była taka –
opowiadali nadoraz sąsiadkowej
więc powtarzam to co nam mówią.
Rodzice – młode małżeństwo –
Tunika – to pierwsze ich dziecko.
po ucieczce z getta, zabrawszy
dziecko i co było najcenniejszego
znaleźli przytułek u tych
właśnie ludzi, na osadzie
wojskowej – Koupie'c. (ale to
nie osadnicy – kupili tą
chałupę) Tych rodziców
trochę potrzymali a potem

wypędzili (tak mówili) dziecioh
pozostał. Niedocznie to oni przez
ludzi dowiadywali się wtedy
o los swego dziecka. Myśmy
ich nie znali. Gdy całą zimę i
wiosnę, my polacy nie mogliśmy
już nocować w swoich domach
bez narażenia życia, tembardziej
że gospodarswa nane były
pojedyncze - nie wieś, więc i
opiekunowie Ineczki nie nocowali
w domu - uciekali do wsi, ale
dziecko pozostawiali w domu
w kotlinarce. „Może w nocy
banderowcy spalą - skończy
się opieka!" W lutym 43 roku
przejechali całkowicie do Rakowa
Nowa - a 1½ rocie maleństwo
pozostało samo na gospodarce!
3 dni tam leżało bez jedzenia,

i w nieopalanej izbie! Nikt nie
przyniósł; nikt nie spalił drzwon

Gdy po 3-ch dniach przyjechali
dwoiéčnéč nś z Radziwiłłowa
opiekunowie, dom stał, a w
nim malutkie dziecko – żywe!
Wtedy zabrali go już ze sobą
do Radziwiłłowa i zamknęli
w (piwnicy) ciemnej.
My śmy przyjechali w cerwon
43 w roku tu do Rach.
Te szczegóły, to j. o tej zimie,
pod przysięgą nie mogę stwierdzić
bo to opowiadali nam sąsiedzi
tych ludzi – opiekunów,
nazwiska nie chcę wymienia.
Lecz wygląd dziecka, chyba
był dostatecznym świadectwem
że to prawda...

Wracam do chwili w której dowiedzieliśmy się o istnieniu Irmiński – i to
wszystko mogę stwierdzić
przysięgą. Po wyjściu tej roksiny
do Brodów, opowiadała o niej, i
— jakim stanie się znajduje
i gdzie jest — dziewczynkę, która
mieszkała w tym samym domu.
Chciałam wierzyć i powiedziałam
jej, żeby jakoś tak zrobiła, bym mogła
sama zobaczyć to dziecko. Po kilka
dniach przybiega do nas Losia ....
"Proszę iść, zaraz pokaż Sabińce, przyjdzie
Alika (córka opiekunów) zamknęłam
ją z niemcami w pokoju, a panią
puncz do kuchni, gdzie jest Kościółka
z dzieckiem, bo dziś odemknięte."
Tak też się stało, ja, Jema i Nauka
(córki nami nu pałacie wszystkiemu
się do kuchni. Kobo pobyty, w ordp...

puchu – malutkie ćwiartki…
Lośka podbiegła do nich i odemknęła!
Tego co zobaczyliśmy, póki życia
nie zapomnę! Trwoga jęłam, bo
życie nie pieściło mnie od dzieciństwa
lecz coś się koło serca mi zrobiło, że aż
się rozchwiałam i rozpłakałam! Trupek –
jakaś mara: włoski dęba stoją,
oczki – jak gałeczki na wierzchu,
szyjka jak podeszwa – rączki jak paluszki
do góry podniesione, i wszystko to
białe szklisto – wahadłowym ruchem
poruszane, gdy światło padła
przez odemknięte ćwiartki – oczków
nie zamknęła, ty Dno coś zabełta…
nie wiem, może to już moja wyobraźnia
bo wydało mi się, że zawołało „mamo”
ale chyba się wydało, bo nie musiała jęknąć
mówić, gdyśmy zabrali ją do siebie.
Pod jakim wrażeniem wróciłyśmy

do domu, nie będą pisało — ale co robić?
Ratujmy się z mężem i dziećmi —
dzieci wszystkie — brać! A my?...
dwa wyjścia: — brać — narazić się
całą rodziną, a kto był w te czasy
wie co to znaczyło! Pozostawić w
takim stanie, na pastwie konania
z głodu, tuż obok nas — nie można!
Iść do gestapo — niech rozstrzelają?
Nie mamy prawa — toż to człowiek —
maleńki człowieczek, nic nikomu
złego nie zrobiło to maleństwo!
Tego nie zrobimy, nie sprawimy
sobie sami jego niewinną krwią!
Jednem słowem mąż zadecydował:
„Co Bóg da — zabrać dziecko do
nas." A ja w duchu dodałam
„Może Bóg ulituje się i ześle nam
tam gdzieś znajdzie dobrych ludzi
którzy się nią zaopiekują."

Pan Bóg dał ją nam w ręce, więc wierzę
że uda się nam ułożyć jej życie
aby było dobre.
Na tem kończę tą historję Tunoki
i dla niej to piszę.
A gdy pomyślę, że będę zmuszona
ją oddać, b. ciężko się robi, ale
tak boję się, aby jej życie późniejsze
nie było zbyt ciężkie w naszem
otoczeniu, naturalnie nie w
rodzinie bo prócz serca i pieniędzy
nic jej nie otacza.

APPENDIX 2

The Diary of Stanisława Roztropowicz

July 11, 1943

Today at around 10 am, our house was burned down. Olek K. passed by the house while it was burning, and the fire spread to other buildings. What shall we do now? Will we be able to go over to our farm, where we grow vegetables, grain and fruit, etc…? And what will happen if we can't? I don't know.

Another big change has occurred in our family: we are now six, not five like before. The sixth person is Sabina. We call her Inka. She is a two-year-old baby girl. She has blonde curly hair and big blue eyes; her eyes look even bigger because she is so thin. She has just had a bath and is dressed in a clean outfit; she is lying down in her crib. She won't sleep, she just cries. Usually she is very quiet; she plays by herself, and doesn't whine. Her conditions are ideal compared to what she was living in before. She doesn't have a lot of clothes. She has a coat, a sweater, three dresses, two shirts, and shoes. Kazik S. passed by today and saw our Inka. He started to ask where we got her. Our mother told him something, but not the whole truth. Kazik left. Minutes later, he returned with a blue dress and an undershirt. The blue dress is very pretty.

July 14, 1943

Today Inka is smiling – the first time since she came to live with us. We are like children when Inka starts laughing; we start laughing, too. In other words, Inka is wonderful. She is also wonderful because she urinated all over me; not only that, she did something worse! My mother returned a minute ago, shar-

193

ing with us the news she heard in town. Oh, Inka is taking a bath; we have to check on her.

July 20, 1943

In the last few days there's been only one violent incident: they burned down the farm that belongs to the Ludzi family, nothing else. Tonight our father is planning to go to the farm. We are out of wood; there is a lot of wood out at the farm. Inka is doing well. She is usually quiet; sometimes she cries. She likes my mother the best. She is not afraid of my father.

July 23, 1943

Oh God, oh God! I hope the rumors that are circulating are false. They say that our friends Olek K. and Mietek P. have been killed. It is very upsetting! Wacek's cart came back empty apparently, but I think it had transported some-one injured or dead. Jana and Jendryk saw a man's shoes. Our mother went to see what happened. It is very unsettling. She returned, and is now sitting and crying. Richard Sinkiewicz is dead. He died in the hospital.

When we returned from the farm, Mother was upset. She screamed at us and scolded Father, telling him he shouldn't have sent us alone to the farm. Now Inka is sitting on my lap. She is moving constantly. She is very lively. She has enough clothes.

August 5, 1943

This afternoon Jana, Lida, Inka and I all walked to the lake. Actually, we went to the river. It is crowded and hot. We found an empty spot and sat down. On the way back, we visited the Kopciow family. The elderly Mrs. Kopciow of-fered us baked apples. She also gave us some bread. We thanked her. I wish she had given us some honey!

August 12, 1943

Great news: Inka started to walk! Yesterday she tried for the first time. She walks very funnily, like a duck.

August 16, 1943

Our mother received a card from the Arbeitsamt. It is a work summons.[13]

Luckily, Jana and I are not registered. If we were, they would certainly not have left us alone, because of our age (16 and 17 years old). I don't know how Mother will get out of it. The fact that she is a housewife and has two minors – Jendryk and Inka – might work in her favor.

August 21, 1943

The murders do not stop. The Bandera Ukrainian bandits, who collaborate with the Nazis, beat people up without discrimination. They threaten people that are close to us. Three days ago, they took Basia Borocky and threatened the Tarnawski family. Four days ago they killed a few people, all of them Poles. Meanwhile, God is watching over us. My father brought all the grain home. Today he went to the farm twice. Old Kasia dug up some potatoes. Mother does not let us ride to the farm with him. She thinks it is too dangerous.

August 25, 1943

A terrible heat wave! No rain in sight. This afternoon the sky got cloudy, but now it is clear. Inka is not letting me write. Something has happened to her today; she doesn't want to sleep.

Today we received a letter from Zosia, our oldest sister who was sent to forced labor in Germany. She writes that she is not well. She has trouble with her toe because of all the hard work, and for what? For the rationed food stamps they get? They can't buy anything anymore. There are many refugees from Hamburg there now. She gave her food stamps to the refugees. Zosia writes that wives arrived without husbands, the children without mothers; in short, horrible! Now every morning, at 5 am services are held in our church,

13 The Arbeitsamt was the local German Labor Office, which was set up by the German civilian administration in occupied territories. Before they were murdered, Jews would be drafted for forced labor (usually unpaid) within Poland, whereas local non-Jews would receive notices in the mail ordering them to report to a certain location to be shipped to forced labor in Germany. [ed.]

with people praying to God for peace in the world. Even the Germans have had it with the war, but no end is in sight.

August 26, 1943

I can't say I am comfortable writing. Inka is sitting on my knees. She wants to be held; she is very stubborn.

August 31, 1943

The Hungarian soldiers caught three Bandera fighters.[14] During an investigation they confessed that their colleagues were planning another terror attack on Poles living in Ukraine. Everyone is on alert. Some believe the rumors, others don't. Our mother does not believe the news, but she is very nervous. Our father doesn't know what to think. We did not talk about it. Me, I don't know – I'm not ruling anything out. I try not to get upset by all the talk. There is a tense atmosphere everywhere. It is not a happy atmosphere, but life goes on.

Tonight there was a scandal with Inka. She didn't want to say goodnight to everyone. Twice our mother put her in a dark room. Inka cried, coming to the door, and putting her fingers in the keyhole. Finally our mother asked her, "Will you be good?" and she answered, "Yes." Our mother asked her, "Do you want me to hold you?" Inka ran and jumped into my mother's arms. Mother said: "Will you say goodnight to everyone now?" Again, Inka said, "No!" This scene was repeated several times. At last, she said goodnight to the family very sweetly. In return she got kisses and hugs from everyone, especially from Mother.

Our mother used this incident to teach us how not to let your children have the last word. It is not always easy to discipline your child. It was advice given way too early!

Today was a German funeral. There was a big procession. Apart from the German funeral, there were two [Eastern] Orthodox funerals. One Ukrainian died; a piece of the Jewish ghetto wall fell on him.

14 Parts of this area of prewar Poland that were annexed by the USSR in 1939 and invaded by Germany and its allies in June 1941 were under Hungarian occupation at this time. [ed.]

September 8, 1943

Wednesday, the holy birth of Mary: the atmosphere is not festive. Zosia Stramska came over, and we played a game called "1,000." Later, Inka and I went to her house. Then we returned, and now I am writing.

On Sunday night, Bandera's bandits took a Polish family from Radziwiłłów away with them. Not from the city itself, but from a suburb called Balek. They came at night. Fearing they could cause alarm with gunshots, they did not kill them on the spot, but took them with them. The family's corpses were found close to Baran.

Again, there are rumors about an attack on Radziwiłłów. Today the rumors subsided. It's like an enormous blackbird spread its wings over the city, and a terrible fear engulfed everyone. It then disappears, only to reappear in a different form.

September 8, 1943

The uproar caused by the priest who left our town finally dissipated. Those who planned to leave town decided to wait. Our mother went to Brody to take care of personal matters. She returned the day before yesterday. She said that the decision to leave town is final. Tomorrow is Sunday; for the first time there will be no sermon in church.

It is evening. Inka is sleeping. We had so much fun with her today. Just before dinner, Jana put her on the potty. She was holding a pancake in her hand. I was in the kitchen. All of a sudden, I heard Inka shrieking. I ran out to the garden and this is what I saw: Inka sitting on the potty with her hands in the air. She was holding the pancake up and screaming at the top of her lungs, while Puchcia the chicken was trying to snatch the pancake from her hands.

September 8, 1943

Some of the army left Radziwiłłów. Another unit is supposed to take their place. The headquarters is already here. There is a plan to give our third room to a German soldier. It will make us safer.[15]

---

15 When the Germans occupied an area, many private homeowners were asked to house German soldiers. This could also make that particular home safer for its inhabitants.

September 24, 1943
Today a German officer moved in with us. He is tall and slim.

October 15, 1943
This is the second day that our officer is gone. We have changed our negative opinion of him. He has come home rarely, only two or three times. He is intelligent. His superior is from Austria – he has come to our home several times. He gives Inka candies frequently.

October 19, 1943
Yesterday Mr. D. went to Brody. There was a package for us from Zosia; Mr. D. is so absentminded that he forgot the package! He leaves tomorrow. We should have the package the day after tomorrow. Some workers arrived, all men, from Ukraine. They are in terrible shape. They are filthy, unshaven, and with ragged clothes.

October 22, 1943
Zosia sent a shirt for Inka, a little sugar, some tissue paper, some cigarettes and two belts. We still don't know who the workers in the ghetto are.[16]

October 23, 1943
Stryj Kazio was murdered. May he rest in peace. There were two Stryjows, and both were murdered – one by the Soviets and one by the Ukrainians.

November 3, 1943
Yesterday Jana, my friend Zosia Stramska and I went to the cemetery to clean the tombstones of Polish soldiers and murdered people with no family. It was quiet and calm; you could hear the movement of the trees. In the afternoon, we

---

16 The Radziwiłłów ghetto was liquidated in October 1942. It is not clear to which workers in the ghetto this sentence refers.

got some flowers and five candles. We were placing flowers on the tombstones of Polish soldiers who had died between 1849 and 1863, when we noticed three Hungarian officers. They walked over to a tombstone from 1863, saluted and knelt down. Our mother and Inka were standing there. Mother advised us to light a candle on the tombstone of the Hungarian soldiers. After the ceremony, they put a wreath on the graves of the Hungarian soldiers. Then they came over to the grave of our Polish soldiers and repeated the same ceremony. Mother thanked them. They shook hands with us. We were very grateful to them for the respect they showed to our soldiers. We will always remember them.

November 13, 1943

The Germans are retreating in the west. We hear horror stories about their retreat. Only the sky and the earth remain intact; they destroy everything along their way. The Germans are demanding more Polish homes for their pilots, who will be arriving shortly. Ms. Alina had to give up one room, and Ms. Janina had to give them two rooms and a hallway. That is how it is everywhere.

November 30, 1943

We are sitting at home with Ms. Alina. She is resting, lying down, while Herr Otto is playing his harmonica. Herr Otto is the German pilot assigned to Ms. Alina's house. At the dinner table were Ms. Anna Tereska and other out-of-towners staying here. After dinner, Herr Otto played the harmonica. Everyone left before 7 pm because of the curfew.

Inka ate her dinner early, before us. Mother put her to bed. She was so playful. She didn't want to sleep and ended up staying up with us to the end. While Herr Otto was playing, she was playing on her own toy harmonica. She looked very funny. Her harmonica doesn't make any sound, but she was convinced that she was playing. It was a delightful scene! A little Jewish girl entertaining a German!

November 18, 1943

You can feel the Front in the air. The Soviets are now in Zhtomir [Żytomierz]. Today the Germans seized a few people.

They were digging trenches. I don't feel afraid. Different rumors are circulating, some of which can make you cry and others might make you laugh.

Our photos are ready. They took a picture of Inka with her dolls. She laughed and was fidgety all the time. Finally, the photographer said, "Look, a birdie!" Inka's mouth opened and she looks like a real dope!

December 15, 1943

We just received a letter from Germany from our oldest sister, Zosia. She writes that this year nobody will get vacation time. A great change has occurred in her life, a change for the better. They transferred her to work in the household of a Catholic priest.

She gets good food and her own warm room. He has only one cow, ten rabbits and a dog. She cleans the kitchen and sometimes she also cleans the priest's room.

December 24, 1943

Christmas Mass is over. The holidays went by so fast! Ms. Alina came for dinner. They left with Jana around 8 pm. Soon after that, three Germans arrived: two familiar, the third we didn't know. Mother played the gracious hostess. My youngest brother Jendryk is already asleep, and so is Inka.

December 29, 1943

It is almost the end of the year. The Germans took over another part of the house, so we moved out of the bedroom and into the kitchen. It is very crowded. We moved two beds into the kitchen. Mother and Inka sleep on one and Jendryk on the other.

January 1, 1944

New Year is here! It is evening. Jendryk and Inka are asleep. Mother is in the kitchen; Father is talking to Szkroba. Mother is trying to find him living quarters. He can't stay here because too many Germans come to our house.

Szkroba was a Ukrainian who cooperated with the Soviet regime before the German occupation. He was hiding from the Ukrainian nationalists, who murdered his entire family.

January 7, 1944

Eleven people are going to sleep in our house!

January 9, 1944

Our company left yesterday at 10. They were Volksdeutsche from Rovno [Równe; Rivne]. They have every reason to flee from the Soviets. Yesterday the Germans moved into our house. They are expecting more German troops to arrive in Radziwiłłów. Szkroba will be leaving our place soon.

Today is Sunday. After breakfast I went with Mother to help the Polish poor and needy. I passed the afternoon reading. Later on, I went with Jana and Inka to visit Ms. Anna. It is now after dinner: Father is reading, Jendryk and Inka are sleeping, Szkroba is dreaming, and I am translating German textbooks.

January 20, 1944

The mood has changed and we all are calmer; we have postponed our departure. The Front has moved away from us. Jana did not recover completely from the flu. Inka is still sick, but she seems to be feeling better this afternoon.

February 13, 1944

It is evening. It is the third day without electricity. Mother and Inka are asleep. Father is reading. I am writing. We don't have any candles. We use an oil lamp, but it doesnt last for very long. We end up going to bed early.

March 19, 1944

A historic date to remember: March 19, 1944 – the Soviets re-conquered our city. We watched the German troops leave and the Soviet soldiers sneak into the back of the houses.

March 30, 1944

We were sure that the front would pass through in two or three days. As it turns out, we have been on the front line for the last two weeks, and there is no end in sight. Between Brody and Radziwiłłów there is a huge forest that the Soviets are unable to conquer. The shooting does not stop. Our apartment near the asphalt is in ruins. It happened last week. Now we live in an apartment near Krzemieniecka Street. There are Soviet anti-aircraft missiles near our old apartment. The first time they used them, I became really frightened; I thought they were bombing us. Later we stood in front of the house and watched the battle. It was an incredible sight, wonderful and horrible at the same time. We saw a fireball in the air and then clouds of black fumes. It was nothing in comparison to the time we were bombed. When the first bombs fell we were in the apartment. There are no windows in our house anymore; everything is covered with dust and black ashes, and what unbearable noise! We heard the planes; we were certain they were Soviet. Only when they were above us did the bombing begin. The bullets started flying above our heads. After the first bomb, the anti-aircraft went into action. We ran into the trenches dug by the Soviets near our house the other day. The noise of the planes and the explosion of the bombs caused the earth around us to tremble. Sand from the trenches fell on our heads. Inka was screaming. Soviet soldiers were jumping into the trenches, practically onto our shoulders. Mother was trying to calm Inka down. The Soviet soldiers said, "Let her scream, nobody can hear her anyway!"

When it was all over, we could not live in the house anymore; we had to move to a new place.

April 12, 1944
Evacuation! An officer just came in to notify us.

April 16, 1944
It is our third day in Bialokrynicy, about 5 km. from Radziwiłłów. We left on Wednesday; today is Sunday. We live in the run-down house of Stefan Stramski. Mother is very upset with a Ukrainian family named Majewski who trashed the place. Inka requires lots of care; we get up several times at night to take care of her. She is prone to colds.

The first night, Mother and Inka slept on the kitchen floor; the next night, the two decided to move into the messy "living room" with us. We spread our belongings on top of smelly fertilizer. Mother, Inka and Father – we all slept there.

May 14, 1944
We are in Dubno, 60 km. from Radziwiłłów. All our belongings are on two carts. Father, Gustek, Jana and Marysia are on the first one, and Mother, Inka and I – and of course the cow – are on the second.

In Dubno, Jendryk and I started attending school. Jana began working in school as a secretary, and Inka is growing up healthy and safe.

August 27, 1944
I decided to look at my diary again after quite a while, out of boredom. I have nothing to read; I don't feel like drawing. Father is reading; Jendryk went to

look for a tire for his bike. Mother took Inka to a P.T.A. meeting, where she is presiding.

January 16, 1945
Warsaw is liberated! The Germans are retreating; the Allies are on the offensive!

April 3, 1945
It's the third day of Easter. We'll be leaving on Easter Saturday. Father got all our belongings onto the railway ramp.

April 20, 1945
I am sitting in the wagon. We'll be leaving soon. We have been sitting in the wagon since noon.

April 27, 1945
A minute ago we arrived at Dzialdowo, on the border with [East] Prussia. We have been traveling for eight days. I have lost track of time; where are we going? We don't know. For sure we'll end up in Prussia.

May 23, 1945
Nidzica. I am in our new home alone with Inka. Mother went to pick up a letter from Zosia. Father went with Jendryk to take some grain to the mill. Jana is working in the repatriation offices.

June 9, 1945
Today I am going to the office. Father and Jendryk and Inka are staying at home.

July 2, 1945
Zosia returned from Germany! It's her second day at home. We are all together at last!

Translated from the Polish by Sabina Heller

PHOTOS AND DOCUMENTS

**Letter from Teresa, of the Lodz orphanage staff,
to Natalia Roztropowicz, 1949**

Kochana pani.

Bardzo panią przepraszam że tak długo
nie odpisałam bo miałam bardzo dużo
roboty teraz jestem na urlopie i mogę
Ineczka zupełnie nic nie płakała
Ineczka przyszła do mnie rano do
kuchni i pytała się czy mamusia
wyjechała. jak powiedziałam że tak
to uśmiechnęła się i wyszła
z kuchni i bawiła się z dziećmi.
Kilka dni tem ja pytałam
się czy chciała by pojechać do
mamusi a ona powiedziała mnie
tu jest bardzo dobrze i niechcę
jechać. Ja bardzo się zdziwiłam
na bardzo dziwny karakter
bo niebyło jeszcze takiego dziecka
któreby nie płakała za mamusią

ten pan co ją przyniósł kupił i
bardzo ładną lalkę a ona chodzi
jest bardzo wesoła tak jak by
się tam urodziła i wyrosła.
Kiedyś przyszła pani kierowniczka
i mówiła pani tereso jakie to jest
grzeczne dziecko niepłacze za domem
nie tęskni więc niech się pani nie
martwi onią bo jej jest tu bardzo
dobrze a każdy ją lubi
dlatego że jest taką grzeczna.
Pozdrawiam panią serdecznie
proszę nie gniewać się że tak
prędko niepisałam Teresa
Proszę nie pisać na adres
do Ledri tylko na adres mojej
matury. Rozalia Halkiew.
Chorzów III.
ul. Rodziewiczówny i 4. m 1.

Letter from Stefania Halkow to Natalia Roztropowicz updating Natalia regarding Inka's departure to Israel, Lodz, August 17, 1950

Łódź, dn. 17. VIII.50

Szanowna Pani!

Zdziwi to Panią bardzo, że po tak długim czasie odpowiadam na Pani list. Mam tak mało czasu że trudno mi nawet oderwać się na chwilę od pracy. A więc co się tyczy Inczki. Ona już od kilku miesięcy jest w Palestynie. Będąc jeszcze tutaj czuła się u tych państwa doskonale. Zrobili dla niej wszystko co było w ich mocy. Miała ona dziewczynę która przez cały dzień się nią zajmowała. Prócz tego mieli również kucharkę. Tuse prze- tłumaczyli że są rodzicami a dziecko takie przecież łatwo można przekonać. Muszę Pani też napisać że wogóle nie miała ochoty pisać do domu listu. Ja byłam u pani doktór to znaczy u tej pani która ma Tukę to powiedziała że nie życzy sobie tego żebym dawała jakikolwiek informacje tyczące dziecka, gdyż ona na- prawdę już zupełnie się u nich zaaklimatyzowała. Ja to również zaobserwowałam. Widywałam ją często gdy ją

dziewczyna do szkoły odprowadzała.
Wyglądała naprawdę bajecznie.
Może Pani być zupełnie spokojna
o los Juki ona ma szczęście
zapewnione. A Pani spełniła
naprawdę święty obowiązek.
Bóg Pani jeszcze za to poświę-
cenie należycie wynagrodzi.
Ja się Jursi nie dziwię, że
ona tak szybko zapomniała
to przecież jeszcze dziecko a tym
bardziej że los nią tak szczęśli-
wie pokierował.
Jeśli będzie w mojej mocy to
chętnie postaram się o adres
Juki. Pani kierowniczka z
którą p. Pani rozmawiała prze-
bywa teraz w Paryżu, oczekuję
tam przyjazdu nieraz. Jeśli

ona pojedzie do Palestyny
to do mnie napisze, może
wtedy przez nią dowiem się
adres Juczki. Sądzę że z
Palestyny pani doktor chętnie
do Pani napisze jak również
Juczka, to już nie będą mieli
się czego obawiać.
Ja mam ciągle listy od mojego
małego, powodzi im się świetnie.
W Palestynie są dzieci naprawdę
otoczone wyjątkową opieką.

    Na tym kończę i pozostaję
        z należnym szacunkiem

                Stefania Malków
Pozdrowienia dla rodziny
Proszę o mnie pamiętać.

"To my beloved Daddy on his saint's day from Inka," March 16, 1946

Portrait of Ina for Daddy, from Inka, March 12, 1949

Koordynacja confirmation of Inka's arrival at the orphanage, Lodz,
October 19, 1948

THE JEWISH AGENCY
Search Bureau for Missing Relatives
P. O. B. 92 Jerusalem

הסוכנות היהודית לארץ־ישראל
המדור לחיפוש קרובים
ת. ד. 92 ירושלים

Phone 231746 .טל

Jerusalem 20.2.92 ירושלים

S. Rostropowicz Stanka
00-116 Warszawa
Świętokrzyska 32 m 32
Poland

Your Ref No. : מספרכם

Our Ref No. 062/ : מספרנו

Subject: Kagan Sabina : הנדון

In answer to your request
dated 2.2.92
we regret to inform you that
so far, all our efforts to trace
the enquiree had no positive
results.

We shall however advise
you immediately of any information we shall receive in the
future.

Your faithfully,

Search Bureau for Missing Relatives

Remarks: Unfortunately we didn't
find her. Maybe she got
another family name

בתשובה לפניתך מיום
הננו מצטערים להודיעך. כי כל מאמצינו
עד כה למצוא את המבוקש(ת) נשארו
ללא תוצאות.

ברגע שנקבל ידיעה כל־שהיא
על הנ־ל נודיע לך.

בכבוד רב,

המדור לחיפוש קרובים
הערות:

Jewish Agency response to Stanka's inquiry, February 20, 1992

From left: Zygmund and Sophia Goszczewski, Inka and Erna, our houseguest, on the balcony of our appartment on 11 Sprinzak Street in Tel Aviv, 1953

Andrzej (Jendryk), Jana and Stanka Roztropowicz, Zdisław Krajewski (Jana's husband), Inka; seated: Ola Roztropowicz, at Andrzej's ranch, Boszowice, July, 2000

Zosia Stramska and Jana Roztropowicz Krajewski, Warsaw, July, 2000

From left: Ola Roztropowicz, Inka, Zosia Stramska and Jana Roztropowicz
Krajewski, at Stanka's appartment in Warsaw, following
the Righteous Among the Nations Award Ceremony, July, 2000

Sabina's sons, Ron and Mark Heller

Inka and Rachel Rabin, 2000